P9-CMA-390

Every recipe in this book gives information on:

– the **number of servings**
– the **preparation time, including cooking time**
– the **nutritional value** per portion

The following symbols are used:

■	= simple
■ ■	= more complicated
■ ■ ■	= demanding

kcal	= kilocalories (1 kcal=4.184 kJ)
P	= protein
F	= fat
C	= carbohydrate

NB.   1 gram protein contains about 4 kcal
        1 gram fat contains about 9 kcal
        1 gram carbohydrate contains about 4 kcal

All temperatures are given in Fahrenheit and refer to the settings used on conventional electric ovens.

– If you have a fan-assisted oven, the temperatures given should be reduced by 85°F.

– Times and settings for microwave ovens are only given in the section on microwave recipes.

SOUPS & SAUCES
CASSEROLES

RECIPES AND PHOTOGRAPHY

INTRODUCTION TO BROTHS, SOUPS & SAUCES

– Friedrich W. Ehlert –
– Odette Teubner, Kerstin Mosny –

HEARTY HOME COOKING

– Rotraud Degner –
– Pete Eising –

DISHES FROM AROUND THE WORLD

– Rotraud Degner –
– Ulrich Kerth –

COOKING FOR SPECIAL OCCASIONS

– Marianne Kaltenbach –
– Rolf Feuz –

WHOLEFOOD RECIPES

– Doris Katharina Hessler –
– Ansgar Pudenz –

QUICK-AND-EASY RECIPES

– Cornelia Adam –
– Michael Brauner –

MICROWAVE RECIPES

– Monika Kellermann –
– Odette Teubner, Kerstin Mosny –

LEAN CUISINE

– Monika Kellermann –
– Volker Goldmann –

Translated by UPS Translations, London
Edited by Josephine Bacon and Ros Cocks

CLB 4217
Published originally under the title
"Das Neue Menu: Eintöpfe, Suppen und Saucen"
by Mosaik Verlag GmbH, Munich
© Mosaik Verlag, Munich
Project co-ordinator: Peter Schmoeckel
Editors: Ulla Jacobs, Cornelia Klaeger, Heidrun Schaaf, Dr Renate Zeltner
Layout: Peter Pleischl, Paul Wollweber
English translation copyright © 1995 by CLB Publishing, Godalming, Surrey, UK

Published in the USA 1996 by JG Press
Distributed by World Publications, Inc.
All rights reserved. No part of this book may be reproduced or transmitted in
any form or by any means, electronic or mechanical, including photocopying,
recording, or by any information storage and retrieval system, without
permission in writing from the Publisher.
Printed and bound in Singapore
ISBN 1-57215-078-5

The JG Press imprint is a trademark of JG Press, Inc.
455 Somerset Avenue
North Dighton, MA 02764

SOUPS & SAUCES
CASSEROLES

JG PRESS

Contents

Whether you are making a delicate, clear consommé for a festive occasion or preparing a more substantial family meal, all soups and stews start from the same basis – the broth. Of course, granules and cubes may be used, but their flavor cannot compare with the home-made variety. With the right instructions, making your own broth is easy. Many sauces require a similar base – a concentrated form of broth. This, too, is easy to make from meat or fish bones. In fact, the basic ingredients for making sauces are even more varied than those used in making soups; for example, a huge variety of sauces can be produced from a basic mixture of butter and eggs.

This chapter describes the basic techniques and main ingredients required to make broths, soups, and sauces.

SOUPS AND BROTHS

Soups play an important part in any meal. They stimulate the digestive juices, assuaging the initial pangs of hunger without being filling, and simultaneously serve to whet the appetite.

Those who are unwell or convalescing often find that soup is the only food that is both digestible and fortifying (the best soups for those with stomach complaints are the cream and puréed varieties.) Soup is usually eaten as the first course of a meal. If a cold appetizer is served, the soup usually follows it.

THE DIFFERENT TYPES OF SOUP

Soups may be divided into various categories according to the method of preparation:

Broths that are enriched and clarified with meat and vegetables are known as *strong broths* (double-strength broths.) *Simple broths* (consommé) are clear soups that have not been clarified.

Thickened soups may be prepared in various ways. *Cream soups* are thickened with flour, rice, or rice flour and finished off with cream. *Veloutés* are thickened with egg yolk and cream, which gives them a velvety texture. *Purée soups* are thickened with potatoes, vegetables, or pulses and often have cream added to them.

Chilled sweet soups consist mainly of fruit and/or dairy products. **Chilled fruit soups** are thickened with cornstarch, arrowroot, potato starch, sago, or tapioca, while chilled soups made of dairy products are thickened with egg yolk or served unthickened (chilled buttermilk or yogurt soups.)

THE BASIC INGREDIENTS FOR SOUP

The basic ingredient for all soups is the broth, which is made from meat, poultry, game, fish, shellfish, or from the bones or shells.

Meat Bones
Beef bones It is best to use the bones from the leg.
Veal bones have more cartilage than other bones, so they are particularly good for thickening broth.
Bones from other meats, such as lamb, pork, game, rabbit, and poultry, are also suitable for preparing broths, sauces, and soups.

Chicken
Chicken gives broth an especially strong flavor. The best chickens to use for making soup are older hens approaching the end of their laying capacity. These have fairly dry flesh, but are not universally available.

Shellfish and Crustaceans
Lobster, crab, crayfish, shrimp, and small edible shellfish are excellent for making broth. It is not always necessary to use the whole fish; in general, the shells, whether raw or cooked, are sufficient. It is essential, however, that they are completely fresh.

CLARIFYING BROTH

Coarsely ground, lean but gristly beef – preferably knuckle – or ordinary finely ground, lean beef are used to clarify broth. The meat is combined with raw egg white and envelops the cloudy particles in the broth to produce a clear consommé. To ensure that no flavor is lost, add finely-chopped vegetables at the same time as the meat and egg white.

As an alternative to beef, the following may be used: game, lean game trimmings and tendons, or fish and white fish trimmings (excluding the trimmings of eel and fatty fish, such as salmon.)

ADDITIONS TO SOUPS

There are no limits to the imagination here:
Dumplings may be prepared from meat, poultry, liver, fish, seafood, game, beef marrow, or grains.
A variety of **pasta** or **rice,** strips of **pancake,** or simply strips of **meat** add a special touch to any consommé. Vegetables may be diced, sliced, or cut into strips.
Eggs may be added as cooked strips or cooked in the soup itself.
Oysters and other shellfish should be added to seafood soups.

BINDING AGENTS

Cornstarch is used to bind sauces, soups, chilled soups, and sweet dishes. When used properly and cooked for the right length of time, cornstarch, unlike wheat flour, turns completely clear. It binds soups due to its high starch content.
Sago is obtained from the pith of the Asiatic sago palm. It consists of small white balls which turn transparent and gelatinous when cooked. Sago is used for binding strong stocks, chilled soups, and for sweet dishes.
Tapioca comes from South America; it is obtained from the cassava plant and is used in the same way as sago.
Rice flour is snow-white and is suited, above all, for binding veloutés. It contains a large amount of starch, but very little gluten. It is not, therefore, suitable for baking. It has a very limited shelf life.

HOME-MADE BROTHS

At first sight, making your own broth might seem like hard work. However, the effort involved is not really that great and the results are simply unbeatable. The flavor and composition of a home-made broth are far superior to ready-made broth products, such as cubes, granules and canned consommé.

High-quality broth sets when cold. If it is poured into jars while still boiling hot and sealed immediately, it may be kept for several weeks in a refrigerator. Watery broth, on the other hand, is of low quality, lacks strength and aroma, and has a limited storage life.

Freezing broth often removes some of the aroma.

MAKING BEEF BROTH

This basic broth is used for preparing strong broths, soups, and stews.

1. Place the beef bones and a piece of beef in a large pan, cover with cold water, and bring to the boil.

2. Lower the heat so that the water is just simmering. Occasionally skim the froth from the surface of the liquid.

3. Add a handful of washed leek, carrot, and celery; season with garlic, thyme, peppercorns, and a parsley sprig.

4. After 1½-2 hours, the meat will be cooked and can be removed from the broth. If it is not to be used as an addition to the soup, it should be used in another dish.

5. After 2-3 hours, strain the broth through a fine sieve.

6. Once the broth has cooled, skim off the fat from the surface using a skimming spoon or soup ladle. If the froth has been regularly skimmed off the surface of the broth during cooking, and if it has always been kept just simmering, the broth will remain clear. The liquid that is lost through skimming off the froth may be replaced by intermittently adding water.

2.

3.

4.

5.

1.

6.

MAKING CHICKEN BROTH

A basic broth for strong stocks, soups, sauces, and stews.

1. Place chicken trimmings and a large chicken in a pan, cover with warm water, cover the pan, and bring to the boil.

2. Lower the heat, and simmer so that the liquid does not turn cloudy. Occasionally skim the froth off the surface and remove any fat.

3. After 2 hours, add the vegetables (leek, carrot, celery) and the herbs and spices (garlic clove, white peppercorns, a thyme sprig, a parsley sprig.)

4. Simmer the broth very gently for a further 1 hour.

5. When it is cooked, remove the chicken from the broth, preferably with a skimming spoon, and rinse it with cold water. Similarly, remove the chicken trimmings.

6. Pour the chicken broth through clean cheesecloth, carefully remove the fat, and leave to cool.

If the chicken and chicken trimmings are not used as an addition to the soup itself, they may be used in another dish, such as a stew or chicken salad.

2.

3.

4.

5.

1.

6.

VEAL BROTH

This is made in a similar way to chicken broth and the cooking time is almost identical. Instead of chicken trimmings and chicken, veal bones, tendons, and skin are used. Veal broth is both nutritious and neutral-tasting, so it often forms the basis for white sauces and cream soups.

GAME BROTH

This forms a basis for strong game broths and thick game soups, and is also used for making gravy for game dishes.

1. Melt a little fat and gently fry the finely chopped bones and tendons.
2. Add diced carrot and onion, and continue frying.
3. Occasionally add a little liquid, such as water or red wine, and boil until evaporated.
4. Fill the pan with cold water. Bring to the boil, lower the heat, and simmer very gently for about 2 hours.
5. Frequently skim off the foam. Add peppercorns, juniper berries, garlic, thyme, and rosemary, and simmer for a further 1 hour.
6. Rub the broth through a fine strainer. Leave to cool and, if necessary, remove the fat.

2.

3.

4.

5.

1.

6.

PREPARING FISH BROTH

The bones and head (without the gills) of flatfish such as turbot, sole, and plaice, are best for making fish broth. They have a neutral taste, making them suitable for a range of dishes. However, the bones and heads of other fish may also be used for making broth, although this should then be used only for dishes containing the particular fish used. Salmon bones, for example, are not suitable for a general fish broth, but they may be used in making red wine sauces for salmon dishes.
Before preparing a fish broth, it is important to clean the bones and heads thoroughly. It is essential to remove the gills from the heads, and just before use, both bones and heads should be rinsed in cold water.

Fish broth should never be used for dishes containing shellfish or crustaceans, as they will overpower the delicate flavor of the main ingredient.

1. Chop the fish bones and heads roughly and rinse them under cold, running water. Remove and discard the gills from the heads.
2. Drain the bones. Meanwhile, chop a little onion, the white part of a leek, and some celery. Heat a little oil, and lightly fry the vegetables until soft. Add the bones, and fry for a further 3-4 minutes.
3. Pour in a little white wine and top up with the quantity of water specified in the recipe.
4. Bring to the boil and carefully skim off the froth. Add all the seasoning ingredients (such as celery,

garlic, parsley sprig, thyme sprig, and crushed peppercorns), and simmer gently for 30-40 minutes.
Finally, rub the broth through a fine strainer and leave it to cool.

1.

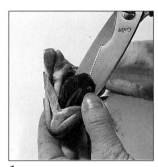

2.

3.

4.

HOW TO CLARIFY SOUPS

In addition to the meat used to clarify the broth, vegetables, such as carrots, leek, and celery, are required. Peppercorns, juniper berries, tarragon, sage, rosemary, thyme, and garlic should also be included, as they add character and flavor to any strong broth, although they should not be too overpowering. The aroma of chicken and game broth is enhanced by the addition of fried chicken or game bones, drained and cooled.

To clarify 1½ quarts broth, you will need:

7 ounces roughly chopped beef, game or fish, depending on the type of strong broth being prepared.
• 1 cup diced vegetables (carrots, leek, and celery).
• 1 egg white. Note: no more than this is required, as too much egg white will impair the taste of the broth.
• For the clarifying mixture, 4-6 tbsps water are needed, plus about 1½ quarts for topping up.
• In the case of chicken or game broth, add about 1 pound fried chicken or game bones.

When making a strong broth:

• The utensils and meat used must be free of fat, as fat impairs the clarifying process.
• The broth used for topping up must not be cloudy.
• Strong broth should be stirred only with a metal spatula until shortly before boiling, so that the egg white does not bind too quickly, or burn and stick to the bottom of the pan.
• Once the liquid has come to the boil, reduce the heat. Keep the strong broth simmering at just below boiling point, and on no account stir it any more.
• Skim the froth from the surface frequently, as it contains fat and impurities.
If the broth does not become clear, strain it, and allow to cool. Prepare a new clarifying mixture and repeat the process. However, the proportion of egg white should not be increased, as this, too, may cause the broth to turn cloudy. Greasy utensils or ingredients may also prevent the strong broth from becoming clear.

PREPARING STRONG BEEF BROTH

1. Coarsely grind the lean beef; alternatively, buy ready-prepared lean ground beef.
2. Wash and chop the carrot, leek, and celery into about ¼-inch cubes.
3. Mix together the meat, vegetables, a few crushed peppercorns, a garlic clove, a parsley sprig, and a little egg white.
4. Add a few tbsps cold water, and knead the ingredients to make a firm mixture.
5. Place in a pan, add the cold broth, and bring to the boil, stirring constantly with a metal spatula.
6. Lower the heat and carefully skim the froth from the surface. Gently simmer the stock for about 2 hours. If too much liquid evaporates, add a little cold water.
7. Rub the strong broth through a fine strainer.
8. Remove the fat from the surface using a coffee filter paper or absorbent kitchen paper. Season with salt, freshly ground black pepper, and a pinch of grated nutmeg.
Double-strength broth is similar to ordinary strong broth, except that twice as much meat is used to clarify it. Very often it is not even necessary to season double-strength broth, as the meat makes it very aromatic. Strong broth tastes delicious both hot and chilled, especially in summer. If you are serving it cold, the broth should set slightly; this is achieved by increasing the quantity of meat and using knuckle of beef, which contains a lot of cartilage.

1.

2.

3.

4.

5.

6.

7.

8.

PREPARING STRONG CHICKEN BROTH

Strong chicken broth is prepared in more or less the same way as strong beef broth.

The precise instructions are as follows:

• Heat a little oil, and fry chicken wings and necks until golden-brown.

• Place them in a sieve to drain.

• Combine coarsely ground clarifying meat, diced vegetables (leek, carrot, and celery), a few crushed peppercorns, a garlic clove, sage leaves, a little water, and egg white to make a solid mixture.

• Place the clarifying mixture in a pan and pour cold chicken or beef broth over it. Bring to the boil, stirring constantly with a metal spoon.

• Lower the heat so the broth is just simmering, and skim the froth from the surface.

• Add the fried chicken trimmings, and gently simmer for about 2 hours.

• If too much liquid evaporates, add a little cold water. When cooked, pour the strong broth through a fine strainer.

• Carefully remove the fat from the surface of the broth using a coffee filter paper or absorbent kitchen paper.

• Season the strong chicken broth with salt, freshly ground black pepper, and a little grated nutmeg. Heat through once more, and serve in heated bowls.

STRONG GAME BROTH

Whatever the type of game, the broth is prepared in the same way as strong chicken broth, although, of course, the meat used is game and fried game bones instead of chicken trimmings. For strong pheasant, partridge, or squab broth, older birds are the best, although their meat is not so good for actual game dishes. This is also true of chicken. The meat of the game bird or soup chicken may be finely diced or cut into strips and used as an addition to the strong broth.

PREPARING STRONG FISH BROTH

Again, the same procedure should be followed:

• Coarsely grind the required quantity of fish (fish trimmings or the flesh of inexpensive fish, but not salmon.)

• Place the fish in a saucepan, with diced white vegetables (leek, celery), a few mushrooms, crushed peppercorns, fresh thyme, garlic, egg white, and a few tbsps water.

• Knead to make a solid mixture.

• Add the cold fish broth, and bring to the boil, stirring constantly.

• Lower the heat, and carefully skim off the froth from the surface.

• Simmer the strong broth gently for about 40-45 minutes. Rub it through a fine strainer.

• Season with salt and freshly ground black pepper, heat through, and serve very hot.

STRONG SHELLFISH BROTH

Strong broths can be flavored with the shells of lobster, crab, crayfish, shrimps or other shellfish. Do not be tempted, however, to top them up with fish broth; it is better to use a neutral broth which will not affect the flavor of the shellfish. Shellfish and fish broth do not go together.

Stale shellfish can be identified by its fishy taste, which indicates a marked loss of quality. This is why fish consommé should not be added to a strong broth made with shellfish; neutral-tasting veal or beef broth should be used. Similarly, beef rather than fish should be used for clarifying. The clarifying mixture should include tomato paste and very ripe peeled tomatoes, as this gives the broth a reddish color. Appropriate meat or vegetables, as well as rice or dumplings, may be added to this strong broth.

SPICES

The aroma of soups and sauces is enhanced by vegetables and herbs and, above all, by spices, which also add color and pungency. Spices are usually added at the beginning of the cooking time. The following list includes some of the most popular spices used in soups and sauces:

Pepper
For broths and soups which require long cooking times, whole peppercorns should be used, as ground pepper loses its aroma more quickly.

Ginger Root
This may be used in both sweet and savory dishes.

Paprika
Often used just for garnishing or adding color.

Chilies
Chilies are available in various sizes and degrees of pungency; they range in color from red to green.

Coriander (Cilantro)
Seeds that have a citrus-like aroma. They are frequently included in curries and are popular in Indian dishes.

Cardamom
A delicious-smelling spice, also used in Indian cuisine.

Juniper Berries
Juniper berries have a pungent taste and are used mainly in savory dishes. They are also used for flavoring gin.

Cloves
Have a very strong aroma and should be used sparingly. They add flavor to filling soups and stews.

Nutmeg
Whether whole or ground, nutmeg is particularly suitable for milk-based sauces. The earlier the nutmeg is added during cooking, the milder it will taste.

Garlic
This is not, in fact, a spice, but a member of the onion family. The aroma of garlic varies depending on how it is used (the quantity and the length of cooking time.)

Curry Powder
A mixture of various Indian spices.

paprika

ginger

curry powder

coriander (cilantro)

cardamom

nutmeg

cloves

chilies

juniper berries

garlic

green peppercorns

pink peppercorns

mustard seeds

white peppercorns

SAFRAN

saffron

black peppercorns

PREPARING CREAM SOUP

To make about 1 quart cream soup, you will need:
½ cup chopped white vegetables (leek, celery, or celery root)
4 tbsps butter
2 tbsps all-purpose flour
3 cups warm broth (fish, chicken, vegetable, veal, beef, or game)
⅓ cup heavy cream
salt
spices

1. Trim and wash the vegetables and peel the celery root, if using. Finely chop them.

2. Melt half the butter over a low heat, but do not allow it to turn brown.

3. Add the vegetables, and gently fry for 2-3 minutes until transparent.

4. Sprinkle with the flour, and gently fry for a further 2-3 minutes. Remove from the heat and set aside to cool slightly.

5. Beat in the broth with a whisk until smooth.

6. Bring to the boil, beating constantly. Lower the heat, and simmer gently for about 20-25 minutes.

7. Add the cream, and bring back to the boil. Season the soup with the spices.

8. Rub the soup through a fine sieve. Gradually beat in the remaining butter, a little at a time.

9. Serve in heated bowls or soup plates. Diced or finely shredded meat or vegetables, dumplings, cooked rice, and chopped herbs, may be added to the soup. The cream soup may be turned into a velouté if it is thickened with egg yolk and cream. To make 1 quart soup, use 1 egg yolk and ⅓ cup heavy cream.

1.

2.

3.

4.

5.

6.

7.

8.

9.

VELOUTÉ SOUPS

Sauces and soups thickened with flour may be brought to the boil without the egg yolk curdling as long as there is no trace of egg white. The proportion of flour can be reduced by about 1 tbsp per quart of soup, as the egg yolk also helps to bind the mixture.

1. Mix together the egg yolk and the cream, and beat in about 1 ladle (½ cup) of hot soup with a whisk.

2. Pour the mixture into the soup, stirring vigorously.

3. Bring the soup to the boil, stirring constantly, then rub it through a sieve.

1.

2.

3.

PREPARING A PURÉE SOUP

For purée soups, any raw or cooked leftover vegetables, potatoes, cooked rice, cereals, and pulses are ideal. If the soup is flavored with a generous quantity of chopped fresh herbs, less salt is needed. Not all purée soups have to be bound with flour or cereal, but this is necessary for those made with vegetables or potatoes, as the liquid might separate from the purée. Once the soup is cooked, toasted breadcrumbs or more, finely chopped vegetables may be scattered on top.

For 1 quart vegetable purée soup, you will need:

1 onion
1 carrot
1 small leek
1 stick of celery
2 tbsps butter
1 tbsp all-purpose flour or cornflakes (as desired)
about 1 quart broth (vegetable, chicken, veal, or beef)
⅓ cup heavy cream
½ garlic clove
salt and freshly ground black pepper
pinch of freshly grated nutmeg

1. Peel and wash the vegetables as required and finely chop them.
2. Melt the butter over a low heat, but do not allow it to turn brown.
3. Add the vegetables, and gently fry until transparent. Sprinkle with the flour, and gently fry for a further 2-3 minutes.
4. Add the broth, and bring to the boil, stirring constantly Simmer gently over a low heat for about 20-25 minutes. Add the cream.
5. Purée the soup with a hand-held mixer or in a blender.

1.

2.

3.

4.

5.

PREPARING SOUP WITH A PUFF PASTRY LID

Using thawed, frozen puff pastry is a quick method of preparing soup with a pastry lid. About 1¼ pounds puff pastry dough is needed for 6 soup bowls.

1. Pour clear soup into 6 ovenproof soup bowls. Beat together 2 egg yolks and a little milk, and set aside.
2. Roll out the dough until it is about ⅛ inch thick. Cut out 6 circles, 1½ inches larger in diameter than the soup bowls.
3. Brush the rim of each soup bowl with the egg-yolk-and-milk mixture.
4. Place a dough lid over each bowl, without stretching it too tightly. Press the edges down firmly to seal.
5. Brush the top with the egg-yolk-and-milk mixture to glaze.
6. Decorate the lid, if desired, and brush the decoration with the egg yolk and milk mixture to glaze.
7. Bake in a preheated oven at 450°F for about 15 minutes.

1.

2.

3.

4.

5.

6.

7.

CHILLED SWEET SOUPS

Chilled sweet soups are a particular specialty of Middle European cuisine, and each region has its own recipes. They are made from fruit, with and without wine, from dairy products, or even using beer.

PREPARING A CHILLED SWEET MILK SOUP

To make 1 quart chilled sweet milk soup, you will need:
2 egg yolks
4 tbsps sugar
½ vanilla pod
1 quart milk

1. Beat together the egg yolks and the sugar until the mixture is creamy.
2. Split the vanilla pod lengthwise, add it to the milk, and bring to the boil.
3. Gradually stir the hot milk into the egg yolk mixture.
4. Return the mixture to the pan and set over a low heat, stirring constantly, until it thickens and coats the back of the spoon. Do not allow the mixture to boil.
5. Set the milk soup aside to cool, stirring occasionally. Strain through a sieve. Serve with berries or almond macaroons.

1.

2.

3.

4.

5.

PREPARING A CHILLED SWEET FRUIT SOUP

Berries, other soft fruits, citrus fruits, or tropical fruits may all be used to make chilled sweet fruit soups. Rhubarb may also be used.

To make 1 quart, you will need:
4 cups prepared fruit
about 2½ cups water
2 tbsps sugar
juice of ½ lemon
1 tbsp sago or tapioca

1. Place the fruit, ⅔ of the water, the sugar, and lemon juice in a pan, bring to the boil and cook until tender.
2. Press or rub the cooked fruit through a sieve.
3. Bring the sago or tapioca and the remaining water to the boil, and cook for about 12-15 minutes or until transparent.
4. Stir the cooked sago or tapioca into the sieved fruit.
5. Place the bowl containing the soup in cold water, and stir frequently as the mixture cools. A chilled fruit soup makes a delicious refreshment on hot summer days.

The best garnishes for this soup are the same fruits as those used to make it, crumbled meringues, or small macaroons. You can also bind the soup with 1 tbsp cornstarch combined with a little cold water.

Strawberries or raspberries can also be used raw in the soup; in this case, only the sugar, lemon juice and sago or tapioca should be boiled in the water. Wine may be added to fruit soups.

If the soup becomes too thick, it may be thinned with mineral water, fruit juice, or wine.

1.

2.

3.

4.

5.

SAUCES

Good sauces are the sign of sophisticated cuisine. The secret of these is a carefully prepared basic sauce, from which many different types can be made.

In addition to the basic gravy there is the basic white sauce which may be prepared from meat, veal, or chicken broth. Béchamel sauce is a basic sauce prepared with milk instead of broth. Hollandaise sauce is a whisked sauce, the basic ingredients of which are egg yolks, butter, and spices. The basic cold sauce, mayonnaise consists of egg yolks, oil, and spices.

BASIC GRAVY

When making a clear, brown gravy, quality begins with preparing the ingredients. The bones, whether veal, pork, lamb, chicken, or game, should be chopped into walnut-sized pieces. This increases their surface area so that they can be fried more effectively to produce both color and flavor. The vegetables used are carrots and onions in a ratio of one to two. Tomato paste and sugar are not absolutely essential, but they enhance the color of the gravy and help make it glossy. Both must be fried with the other ingredients, so that the tomato paste loses its acidic taste and the sugar loses some of its sweetness. Avoid frying for too long, as this will create a bitter flavor.

It is important not to use too much liquid. About 6 cups is adequate for 2¼ pounds bones.

During cooking, the froth must be skimmed off at regular intervals. It consists of fat released from the bones and protein which attracts dirt particles. The liquid should always be kept simmering just under boiling point.

Spices and flavorings should be added about 1 hour before straining.

Basic preparation

1. Heat a little oil, and fry the chopped bones, tendons, and sinews (preferably veal or pork) until golden-brown and shiny.

2. Add the diced vegetables (consisting of ⅓ carrots and ⅔ onions), and fry until golden brown. If necessary, drain off some of the oil.

3. Add the tomato paste and a little sugar, and fry for a few minutes.

4. Add a little liquid, and cook until it has evaporated.

Repeat this procedure 2-3 times, adding liquid and then reducing. This helps to produce color, taste, and glossiness. Add the remaining liquid, and simmer for about 5 hours.

5. Frequently throughout the cooking time, skim off the froth and fat from the surface. Add the spices and flavorings (crushed peppercorns, crushed garlic, a thyme sprig, a parsley sprig, a little leek, and celery) and simmer for a further 1 hour.

6. Strain the cooked gravy through cheesecloth.

7. Carefully remove any remaining fat from the surface. The bones can also be cooked in a pressure cooker. Cover with a small quantity of liquid and cook for about 40-50 minutes.

The gravy may be poured into heated jars while still boiling hot. Seal the jars so that they are air-tight. When cool, store in the refrigerator. The cold gravy should form a thick jelly. Chicken, lamb, and game bones may also be used in the same way to make clear, brown basic gravies. They may be used as they are or as a base to make other gravies.

It is important to make sure that the right gravy is used for a particular meat dish; for instance, do not serve a lamb-based gravy with chicken. Veal-based gravy is an exception to this rule, as its taste is almost neutral, so it may be used as a base for many gravies.

3.

4.

5.

1.

2.

6.

7.

BASIC WHITE SAUCE (VELOUTÉ)

When making this basic sauce, it is important to use the correct proportions of butter and flour. As a rule of thumb, always use the same number of tablespoons of butter as flour. To make 2 cups sauce, about 2 tbsps each of butter and flour are required.

Basic preparation

1. Melt the butter over a low heat, but do not allow it to turn brown.

2. Stir in the flour, and cook, stirring constantly, for a few minutes. Do not allow it to turn brown.

3. Remove the mixture, called a roux, from the heat, and allow to cool slightly. Gradually beat in the warm broth with a whisk until smooth.

4. Return the pan to the heat and, stirring constantly with a metal spoon, simmer gently for about 20 minutes.

5. Add the cream and bring the mixture to the boil. Season with salt, freshly ground white pepper, and lemon juice.

6. Beat together an egg yolk with heavy cream. Stir some of the hot sauce into the egg yolk and cream mixture.

7. Pour the mixture into the hot sauce and bring to the boil, stirring vigorously.

8. This sauce is especially delicious if it is pressed through a fine sieve.

In order to avoid a skin forming, sprinkle melted butter over the surface, or dot butter over the top and spread it over the surface with a fork.

Basic white sauce does not have to be thickened with egg yolk, but this gives it a milder flavor. A creamy chicken sauce should never be thickened with egg yolk. Basic white sauce may be modified in both taste and appearance by adding wine, mushrooms, herbs, various spices (curry or mustard) or concentrated reduced broth. All light-colored basic broths, whether fish, chicken, vegetable, veal, lamb or beef, are suitable for preparing a basic white sauce, depending on the use for which it is finally intended.

BÉCHAMEL SAUCE

A light, basic sauce, which is prepared using milk instead of broth. Preparation is similar to that of basic white sauce:

• Melt the butter, add finely chopped onion, and lightly fry until transparent.

• Sprinkle with the flour, and cook, stirring constantly, for 2-3 minutes. Remove the pan from the heat.

• Bring the milk to the boil, pour it over the roux, and beat the mixture with a whisk until smooth.

• Return the mixture to the heat and bring to the boil, stirring constantly with a metal spoon.

• Add a small onion studded with 2 cloves and ½ bayleaf. Season lightly with salt and boil for about 20 minutes, stirring constantly.

• Season the sauce with more salt, if necessary, freshly ground black pepper and grated nutmeg. Rub the sauce through a fine sieve.

• Sprinkle melted butter over the surface, or dot with butter and spread over the top with a fork.

Part of the milk may be replaced by broth or gravy made from chicken, veal, fish, vegetables, or mushrooms. There are many varieties of béchamel sauce, of which the best-known is mornay sauce. To make mornay sauce, grated hard cheese is added. If used in baking, it is recommended that the sauce is thickened beforehand with egg yolk and cream. This makes it more substantial so that it stays on the surface of the dish to be baked. Another variation of béchamel is white onion sauce.

4.

5.

1.

6.

2.

7.

3.

8.

PREPARING HOLLANDAISE SAUCE

To make 1 cup of this classic whipped sauce, you will need:
¾ cup butter
10 peppercorns
1 onion, peeled and diced
3 tbsps vinegar
3 tbsps water
3 egg yolks
juice of ½ lemon

1. Melt the butter over a low heat until it separates; do not allow it to become too hot. Strain the clear portion of the butter through a fine sieve.

2. To make the reduced liquid, boil the peppercorns and diced onion with vinegar and water, and allow to reduce to about 3 tbsps of liquid.

3. Prepare a bain marie or set a heatproof bowl over a pan of hot water.

4. Place the egg yolks in the bowl of the bain marie. Rub the reduced vinegar mixture through a sieve.

5. Beat together the egg yolks and the reduced vinegar mixture over the hot water.

6. Continue beating the mixture until it is light and creamy and coats the whisk.

7. Stir in the warm, clarified butter, one drop at a time, adding more only when the previous drop has been thoroughly incorporated.

8. Stir in lemon juice, freshly ground pepper, and a pinch of cayenne pepper.

9. The sauce can be made even finer by straining it through cheesecloth.

10. Keep the hollandaise sauce warm. Serve with fish or meat and vegetables.

1.

2.

3.

4.

5.

6.

7.

8.

9.

10.

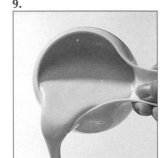

CAUSES OF CURDLING IN HOLLANDAISE SAUCE

- The egg yolks were not beaten thoroughly enough. They should no longer be raw nor taste of raw eggs.
- The egg yolks and the butter were not at the same temperature.
- The butter was beaten in too quickly or too much was added at once.
- The sauce is too thick or contains too much fat.
- The sauce has become too hot or too cold.

WHAT TO DO IF THE HOLLANDAISE SAUCE HAS CURDLED

- Do not stir curdled hollandaise sauce, but pour a little cold water over the surface.
- With an egg whisk, make careful circular movements over a tiny area to combine the sauce. If it starts binding again, enlarge the circles until the whole sauce is smooth again.
- If this method is unsuccessful, depending on the quantity of sauce, a further 1-2 eggs must be beaten.
- Then, instead of the butter, the curdled, warm hollandaise sauce is folded into the eggs.

VARIATIONS OF HOLLANDAISE SAUCE

All these sauces are excellent with broiled meats, fish, and seafood; some also go well with poached fish and vegetable and egg dishes.

Béarnaise Sauce
This differs from hollandaise sauce in that diced shallots, tarragon, chervil sprigs, crushed peppercorns, and white wine are added to the reduced vinegar.

Cedar Sauce
This consists of hollandaise sauce and reduced, fresh mushroom broth.

Choron Sauce
Tomato paste, chopped tarragon, and chervil are added to hollandaise sauce.

Dijon Sauce
Hollandaise sauce with the addition of Dijon mustard.

Maltese Sauce
A hollandaise sauce to which the juice and grated rind of a blood orange are added.

Choron Sauce

Béarnaise Sauce

MAYONNAISE

Mayonnaise is a combination of egg yolks, salt, oil, vinegar, and water. About ¾ cup vegetable oil should be used for each egg yolk.

1. Beat the egg yolks with a little salt until creamy but not frothy.

2. Add the oil, drop by drop, beating it in and only adding more oil when the previous addition has been fully incorporated.

3. If the mayonnaise becomes too thick or will not absorb any more oil, add a few drops of vinegar or warm water.

4. Continue adding the oil in a thin stream until it is used up and the mayonnaise has a thick consistency. Then stir it thoroughly one more time.

5. Season the mayonnaise with salt, freshly ground black pepper, a pinch of sugar, and a little mustard. It should be thick and firm.

VARIATIONS OF MAYONNAISE

Mayonnaise is a basic sauce which may be modified by using other ingredients.

Chantilly Sauce
Season the mayonnaise with lemon juice, salt, and cayenne pepper, then fold in whipped cream. Serve with shellfish, cold artichokes, and asparagus dishes.

Cocktail Sauce
Cocktail sauce is made from mayonnaise, tomato ketchup or chili sauce and whipped cream, seasoned with brandy, salt, cayenne pepper, and lemon juice. Chopped dill or tarragon may also be added. It goes with cocktails and with seafood, or chicken salads.

Green Sauce
Purée part of the mayonnaise with blanched spinach leaves in a food processor or using a

1.

2.

3.

4.

5.

hand-held mixer, then rub through a sieve. Combine the spinach mixture with the remaining mayonnaise and a generous quantity of freshly chopped herbs, before seasoning with lemon juice, salt, and freshly ground black pepper. Serve with fried or poached cold fish, fish and seafood dishes, or cold egg dishes.

Remoulade Sauce
Season the mayonnaise with mustard, then add finely chopped gherkins, capers, anchovy fillets, tarragon, and parsley. Serve with cold meats, cold egg dishes, or fish fried in breadcrumbs.

Tartare Sauce
This consists of a strongly seasoned mayonnaise, chopped hard-boiled eggs, and finely snipped fresh chives. It goes with cold, roast meats, chicken, and egg dishes, and both baked and cold fish dishes.

Tyrolean Sauce
A sharp mayonnaise, mixed with chili sauce, diced tomato, garlic, parsley, and chives. Serve with boiled, roast or cold meats and chicken, with cold egg and shellfish dishes, or with fish.

Gribiche Sauce
The yolks of hard-boiled eggs, rubbed through a fine sieve, are combined with mustard and mayonnaise to make a smooth mixture. Chopped capers, gherkins, cooked egg whites, and herbs are added and the sauce is then seasoned generously with Worcestershire sauce. Serve with cold meat, fish, or eggs.

Hearty Home Cooking

*A*n older generation of cooks can indulge in nostalgia, while the young are keen to return to tried-and-tested recipes – especially when tradition means freshness and spice. After all, who could resist a Spring Vegetable Soup with ingredients bought fresh from the market or, better still, harvested from the garden? Farina dumplings represent the best of Continental home cooking, and with Chicken Soup, they make a delicious appetizer for a Sunday lunch. More substantial dishes include Lentil Stew with Leg of Goose, while the sauces all exemplify the new lightness of home cooking.

Spring Vegetable Soup
(recipe page 32)

31

POTATO SOUP WITH SHRIMP

SERVES 4 ■■
Preparation time: 1 hour
Kcal per serving: 195
P = 12g, F = 9g, C = 16g

8 ounces chicken trimmings
   (wings, neck, giblets)
1 small leek
1 carrot
1 small parsnip
1½ quarts water
salt
4 cups potatoes
2 egg yolks
1 tbsp butter
1 tbsp finely chopped fresh
   root ginger
4 tbsps heavy cream
¾ cup shelled cooked shrimp
1 tbsp chopped fresh dill
1 tbsp chopped fresh parsley

Cook the chicken trimmings, leek, carrot, and parsnip in water for 1 hour.

Bay shrimp are best for the shrimp cream sauce.

Briefly heat the shrimp in the ginger and cream mixture.

Place 2 tbsps of the shrimp cream in each bowl of soup.

1. Wash the chicken trimmings. Wash the leek, and peel the carrot and parsnip. Finely chop the prepared vegetables. Place the chicken and prepared vegetables in a pan, add the water, season with salt, and bring to the boil. Lower the heat and simmer for 1 hour. Strain into a clean pan.

2. Peel and dice the potatoes. Add the potatoes to the broth, bring to the boil, and cook for 25 minutes. Rub the soup through a sieve or purée, using a hand-held mixer. Return to the pan and bring to the boil. Remove the pan from the heat and beat in the egg yolks.

3. Melt the butter in a small pan, add the ginger, and gently fry for a few minutes. Pour over the cream and gently heat through. Add the shrimp and gently heat through without allowing the cream to boil.

4. Pour the soup into individual soup bowls, place 2 tbsps of the shrimp and cream mixture in the center of each, and garnish with dill and parsley.

SPRING VEGETABLE SOUP

(photograph page 30/31)

SERVES 4 ■
Preparation time: 2 hours
Kcal per serving: 205
P = 7g, F = 13g, C = 14g

1¼ pounds veal bones
1½ quarts water
salt
2¼ pounds mixed young
   vegetables (peas, carrots,
   green beans, cauliflower,
   asparagus, kohlrabi, Savoy
   cabbage)
4 tbsps butter
2 tbsps chopped fresh herbs
   (dill, chervil, parsley,
   chives)

1. Wash the veal bones. Place them in a pan, add the water and a pinch of salt, and bring to the boil. Lower the heat and simmer for 1½ hours.

Wash and prepare the vegetables, and cut them into bite-sized pieces or matchstick strips.

2. Prepare the vegetables and cut them into small pieces or slices. Melt the butter in a large pan, add the vegetables, season with salt, and gently fry for a few minutes. Strain the veal broth over the vegetables, and simmer for 30 minutes.

3. Adjust the seasoning if required. Transfer the soup to individual soup bowls and sprinkle with the herbs. Semolina dumplings or strips of scrambled egg may also be added.

BEAN SOUP WITH LAMB

SERVES 4 ■
Preparation time: 2½ hours
Soaking time: overnight
Kcal per serving: 475
P = 34g, F = 19g, C = 42g

1 cup white beans
2 quarts water
1 leek
1 onion
1 small parsnip
2 carrots
1 tomato
3 potatoes
2 savory sprigs
1 thyme sprig
2 sage leaves
½ bayleaf
1 onion studded with 2
   cloves
2 pounds shoulder of lamb
salt
freshly ground black pepper
2 tbsps chopped fresh parsley

1. Wash the beans and place in a bowl. Cover with cold water and set aside overnight to soak.

2. Wash and slice the leek. Peel and slice the onion, parsnip, and carrots. Dice the tomato. Peel and dice the potatoes. Place the beans and their soaking water in a pan, and add the vegetables, herbs, studded onion, and the lamb. Bring to the boil, and skim off any froth that forms. When no more froth forms, season to taste with salt.

3. Simmer over a medium heat for 1½-2 hours. Remove the meat from the pan and set aside. Rub about one-third of the soup through a sieve, then return it to the pan, stirring to mix thoroughly. Cut the meat into bite-sized chunks and return it to the pan. Season with salt and pepper and serve garnished with the chopped parsley.

OXTAIL SOUP

SERVES 4　■ ■
*Preparation time: 3½ hours
Kcal per serving: 565
P = 44g, F = 31g, C = 5g*

2¼ pounds oxtail, thickly
　sliced
salt
freshly ground black pepper
1 leek
2 carrots
2 onions
3 tbsps vegetable oil
1½ quarts meat broth or
　water
1¾ cups red wine
½ bayleaf
2 thyme sprigs
2 parsley sprigs
3 tbsps sherry or Madeira

*Fresh vegetables and oxtail are
the main ingredients for this
soup.*

1. Trim the fat from the
oxtail, wash, and pat dry.
Rub the oxtail with salt and
pepper. Wash the leeks and
cut into matchstick strips.
Peel the carrots and onions
and cut into matchstick
strips.
2. Heat the oil in a large pan,
add the meat, and fry until
browned on all sides. Add
the vegetables, and fry for a
further 5 minutes. Pour over
the broth or water and the
wine, and add the herbs.
3. Cover and cook over a
low heat or in a preheated
oven at 375°F for about 3
hours. Stir in the sherry or
Madeira.

*After frying the meat for a few
minutes, add the thinly sliced
vegetables.*

*Sago is a starch made from the
white part of the sago palm.*

TIP

*Adding a little
sago makes this
soup light and
creamy.*

---

4. Strain the soup and
remove any fat. Cut the meat
from the bones and return it
to the soup. Season with salt
and pepper, pour into a
tureen and serve.

CHICKEN SOUP WITH FARINA DUMPLINGS
(photograph page 17)

SERVES 4　■ ■
*Preparation time: 3 hours
Kcal per serving: 835
P = 52g, F = 60g, C = 22g*

1 small chicken, with giblets
2 quarts water
2 carrots
1 parsnip or turnip
1 leek
1 stick of celery
1 small onion
salt
2 tbsps finely chopped fresh
　parsley

**FOR THE FARINA
DUMPLINGS:**
3 tbsps butter, softened
salt
pinch of freshly grated
　nutmeg
2 eggs
½ cup farina

1. Wash the chicken and the
giblets. Reserve the liver, and
place the chicken and remaining giblets in a large pan. Peel
and coarsely chop the carrots
and parsnip or turnip. Wash
and coarsely chop the leek
and the celery. Peel and
coarsely chop the onion. Add
the vegetables and water to
the pan, and season to taste
with salt. Bring the mixture to
the boil, lower the heat, and
simmer for 2-3 hours. Add the
reserved liver shortly before
the end of the cooking time.
2. Remove the chicken from
the broth. Cut the flesh from
the bones, discard the skin,
and cut the meat into strips.
Strain the broth and skim off
any fat that has formed.
3. To make the farina
dumplings, beat the butter
until it is light and creamy. Add
the salt and nutmeg. Beat the
eggs into the butter, one at a
time. Fold in the farina. Leave
the mixture to stand for 15
minutes.
4. Bring the chicken broth to
the boil. Using 2 wet spoons,

*Cook the whole chicken with the
giblets and vegetables.*

*Fold the farina into the beaten
butter-and-egg mixture.*

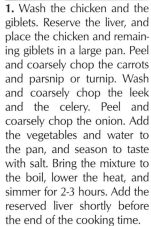

*Shape the dumplings using 2 wet
spoons, then place them in the
simmering chicken broth.*

make a "trial" dumpling from
the dough, and place it in the
soup. If it turns too hard, add a
little more water to the dough;
if it is too soft, add a little more
farina. Shape the remaining
dough into dumplings, and
cook in batches in the simmering broth for 15-20 minutes.
The dumplings will puff up during cooking, so do not pack
them too tightly in the liquid.
5. Return the chicken to the
broth and heat through. Transfer
to individual soup bowls, sprinkle with the parsley, and serve.

TOMATO SOUP WITH MEAT DUMPLINGS

SERVES 4 ■
*Preparation time: 30 minutes
Kcal per serving: 255
P = 13g, F = 18g, C = 10g*

FOR THE SOUP:
*3 cups canned tomatoes
2 slices bacon, rinds removed
1 onion
1 carrot
1 stick of celery
1 tbsp olive oil
1 tbsp chopped fresh parsley
1 oregano sprig or ¼ tsp dried oregano
1 quart water
salt
freshly ground black pepper
knob of butter*

FOR THE MEAT DUMPLINGS:
*½ cup lean ground beef
¼ cup ground pork
1 small egg, lightly beaten
salt
freshly ground black pepper
1 tbsp minced parsley
3 tbsps breadcrumbs
½ tsp grated lemon peel*

1. To make the soup, drain the tomatoes and reserve the juice. Chop the tomatoes.
2. Finely dice the bacon. Peel and finely dice the onion and carrot. Wash and finely dice the celery.
3. Heat the oil in a pan, add the bacon, and fry until the fat runs. Add the onion, carrot, celery, and parsley, and fry for 5 minutes. Add the tomatoes and oregano. Pour in the reserved tomato juice and the water. Bring to the boil, lower the heat, and simmer for 20 minutes.
4. Rub the soup through a sieve, and season to taste with salt and pepper. Return to the pan.
5. To make the dumplings, knead all the ingredients to make a smooth dough. Shape it into small dumplings with wet hands. Place the dumplings in the

Chop the canned tomatoes.

Fry the bacon until the fat runs, then add the diced vegetables.

To make the dumplings, combine all the ingredients using a fork.

tomato soup, and bring to the boil. Lower the heat and simmer for 20-30 minutes, until cooked.
6. Whisk the butter into the soup. If liked, serve garnished with fresh oregano.

POTATO SOUP

SERVES 4 ■
*Preparation time: 1 hour
Kcal per serving: 740
P = 26g, F = 57g, C = 30g*

*1¾ pounds Idaho potatoes
½ head celery
2 carrots
1 parsnip
1 leek
1 large onion
4 slices smoked bacon, rinds removed
1 tbsp vegetable oil
½ tsp ground caraway seeds
1 bayleaf
¼ tsp dried marjoram
salt
freshly ground black pepper
1½ quarts water
4 frankfurters
2 tbsps chopped parsley
1 tbsp snipped chives*

1. Peel the potatoes and cut into ½ inch cubes. Wash and chop the celery. Peel and slice the carrots and parsnip. Wash and thickly slice the leek. Peel and slice the onion. Finely dice the bacon.
2. Heat the oil in a pan, add the bacon, and fry until the fat runs. Add the potatoes, celery, carrots, parsnip, leek, and onion, and fry for 10 minutes, stirring frequently. Add the caraway seeds, bayleaf, and marjoram, and season to taste with salt and pepper. Add the water. and bring to the boil. Lower the heat and simmer for about 45 minutes or until the potatoes begin to fall apart.
3. Rub half the soup through a sieve or purée it using a hand-held mixer. Return the purée to the rest of the soup.
4. Cut the frankfurters into slices. Add to the soup and heat through. Pour the soup into 4 bowls, and serve garnished with parsley and chives.

MUSHROOM SOUP

SERVES 4 ■ ■
*Preparation time: 1 hour
Kcal per serving: 115
P = 6g, F = 5g, C = 11g*

*6 cups fresh wild mushrooms (e.g. oyster mushrooms, porcini, chanterelles)
2 leeks
1 small onion
1 tbsp butter
1 quart meat broth
1 thyme sprig
1 sprig celery leaves
salt
freshly ground black pepper
2 tbsps sour cream
2 tbsps chopped fresh parsley*

1. Wash and trim the mushrooms. Slice the larger ones and halve or quarter the smaller ones.
2. Wash, trim, and thinly slice the leek. Peel and finely chop the onion.
3. Melt the butter in a pan, and gently fry the leek and onion for 5 minutes. Add the mushrooms, and fry for 2-3 minutes. Add the broth.
4. Add the thyme and celery leaves, season to taste with salt and pepper, and bring to the boil. Lower the heat and simmer for 40 minutes. Remove and discard the thyme and celery leaves.
5. Purée the soup in a food processor or blender. Return it to the pan, and stir in the crème fraîche. Bring to the boil and cook for a few minutes to reduce the liquid. Serve garnished with parsley and, if liked, a few fried mushroom slices.

CHILLED AVOCADO CREAM SOUP

SERVES 4 ■
Preparation time: 20 minutes
Cooling time: 30 minutes
Kcal per serving: 435
P = 4g, F = 42g, C = 4g

2 ripe avocados
½ cup white wine
3 cups meat broth
⅔ cup crème fraîche
2 tsps lemon juice
salt
freshly ground black pepper
8 fresh mint leaves

1. Halve and pit the avocados. Peel each half and chop the flesh. In a food processor or using a fork, mix the avocado flesh with the white wine to make a purée.
2. Bring the broth to the boil. Remove from the heat and beat in the avocado purée with an egg whisk. Stir in the crème fraîche and lemon juice, and season to taste with salt and pepper. Chill in the refrigerator for 30 minutes.
3. Cut the mint into strips and stir it into the soup. Croûtons, made from diced white bread fried in oil, and a few thin slices of avocado may be added to each soup bowl.

> **TIP**
>
> *The avocados used to make this cream soup must be fully ripe. Unripe avocados should be wrapped in newspaper and left for 2-3 days in a cool place to ripen.*

Halve the avocados, pit them, and peel the flesh.

Blend the avocado pieces with the white wine to make a purée.

Beat the hot broth into the avocado purée with an egg whisk.

Cut the mint into strips and mix it into the chilled avocado soup.

CHERVIL SOUP

SERVES 4 ■
Preparation time: 30 minutes
Kcal per serving: 55
P = 3g, F = 4g, C = 1g

5 cups chicken broth
4 tbsps chervil
4 tbsps butter
1 tbsp minced parsley
2 egg yolks

1. Heat the chicken broth. Wash the chervil and pick off the leaves. Finely chop the stems, add them to the broth, and simmer for 10 minutes. Strain the broth.
2. Finely chop the chervil leaves. Cream together the butter, chervil leaves, and parsley to make a paste.
3. Bring the soup back to the boil. Remove it from the heat and beat in the egg yolks. Beat in the herb butter, in small pieces, making sure each piece is fully incorporated before adding the next. Serve the soup in 4 bowls, garnished with a few chervil leaves.

> **TIP**
>
> *Chervil is a strong-tasting herb with a slight aniseed flavor – it should be used sparingly. It goes well with parsley.*

Poached quails' eggs, small salmon dumplings, or croûtons may be added to this dish.

ASPARAGUS SOUP WITH VEAL

SERVES 4 ■ ■
Preparation time: 1½ hours
Kcal per serving: 175
P = 31g, F = 1g, C = 12g

1¼ pounds lean veal
1 veal bone
1½ quarts water
salt
freshly ground white pepper
1¼ pounds asparagus
2 parsley sprigs
1 lettuce heart
pinch of mace
pinch of ground ginger
4-8 thin slices of white bread

1. Wash the meat and the bone. Place them in a pan, cover with the water, and bring to the boil. Skim off any froth from the surface, season with salt, and cook for about 1 hour.
2. Carefully peel the asparagus, cut off the tips, and chop the stems. Place the asparagus stems, parsley, and lettuce heart in a pan and add enough veal broth just to cover. Bring to the boil, and cook for 15 minutes. Add the asparagus tips, and cook for a further 5-10 minutes or until all the vegetables are tender.
3. Drain the asparagus stems, parsley, and lettuce, and rub them through a sieve or purée them using a hand-held mixer.
4. Remove the meat and bone from the broth (leaving the asparagus tips), and set aside. Stir the purée into the broth. Remove all fat and gristle from the meat. Dice the meat and return it to the soup. Season with mace, pepper, and ginger. Toast the bread. Place 1-2 slices of bread in each of 4 individual soup bowls and pour the hot soup over them.

PICHELSTEIN STEW

SERVES 4 ■■
Preparation time: about 2½ hours
Kcal per serving: 375
P = 47g, F = 9g, C = 26g

8 ounces brisket of beef
8 ounces breast of veal
8 ounces leg of pork
2 large marrow bones
8 potatoes
2 large onions
3 sticks of celery
4 carrots
2 parsnips
1 leek
1 small Savoy cabbage
2 tbsps vegetable oil
salt
freshly ground black pepper
1 tsp caraway seeds
2 cups meat broth
2 tbsps chopped fresh parsley

A variety of meats and vegetables give this stew its typical flavor.

Remove the marrow from the bones and carefully cut into slices.

Arrange the meat, vegetables and seasoning in layers, and top the marrow slices.

1. Cut the meat into large chunks. Remove the marrow from the bones and cut it into slices. Peel and dice the potatoes and onions. Wash and chop the celery. Peel and slice the carrots and parsnips. Wash and slice the leek. Wash and quarter the cabbage, cut out the central stem and shred the leaves.
2. Heat the oil in a large pan, and fry the meat, stirring frequently, until browned on all sides. Remove the meat from the pan and keep warm. Place half the marrow slices on the base of a flameproof casserole. Cover with alternate layers of meat, potatoes, and vegetables, seasoning each layer with salt, pepper, and caraway.

3. Top with the remaining marrow. Add the broth and cover. Cook the stew over a low heat or in a preheated oven at 350°F for 1½-2 hours. Serve garnished with parsley.

TIP

If you prefer, lamb may be used instead of veal; this will give the stew a stronger flavor.

LENTIL STEW WITH LEG OF GOOSE

SERVES 4 ■
Preparation time: 3 hours
Soaking time: about 2 hours
Kcal per serving: 600
P = 62g, F = 10g, C = 59g

1¾ cups lentils
½ cup red wine
1 quart water
1 tbsp vegetable oil
2 goose legs
salt
freshly ground black pepper
1 leek
1 carrot
1 turnip
1 thyme sprig
2 large tart apples
¼ tsp dried thyme
1 tsp sugar

Tart apples and leg of goose are the special ingredients for this stew.

Brown the goose legs on all sides in oil.

Fry the apple slices in 1 tbsp heated roasting juices.

1. Place the lentils in a bowl and pour the wine and water over them. Set aside for about 2 hours to soak.
2. Heat the oil in a large flameproof pot, and fry the goose legs until browned on all sides. Season with salt, cover, and roast in a preheated oven at 400°F for 1½ hours. Remove the pot from the oven, and transfer 1 tbsp of the roasting juices to a clean pan.
3. Wash the leek and peel the carrot and turnip. Finely chop the vegetables and add to the goose, together with the thyme sprig. Fry over a low heat for a few minutes. Add the lentils with their soaking liquid and stir well. Cover the pot tightly and return it to the oven for a further 45 minutes.
4. Peel, quarter, core, and slice the apples.
5. Heat the reserved roasting juices, and gently fry the apple slices for a few minutes. Sprinkle with the dried thyme and the sugar. Make sure the apple slices do not lose their shape.
6. Remove the pot from the oven and carefully stir the apple into the lentils. The goose legs may also be roasted without a lid and on a higher oven setting for the last 15 minutes; this will make the meat beautifully crisp.

FRESH TOMATO SAUCE

SERVES 4

Preparation time: 20 minutes
Kcal per serving: 180
P = 2g, F = 17g, C = 5g

8 large or 12 medium ripe
tomatoes
⅓ cup butter
10-12 torn large fresh basil
leaves
salt
freshly ground black pepper

1. Blanch, skin, and seed the tomatoes. Dice the flesh.
2. Melt half the butter in a high-sided pan, and gently fry the tomatoes for 5 minutes. Add the basil, and season to taste with salt and pepper. Stir in the remaining butter, a little at a time, ensuring each addition has been fully incorporated before adding the next.
This sauce goes well with fish dishes, pasta, and cooked vegetables.

TIP

The tomato sauce may also be puréed using a hand-held mixer, and then boiled a little to reduce the liquid, before adding the remaining butter.

Make a crosswise cut into the base of the tomatoes.

Dip the tomatoes in boiling water or pour boiling water over them.

Rinse immediately with ice-cold water and peel off the skins

When seeding, cut the tomato through the center and remove the seeds and juice using a teaspoon.

NEW DILL SAUCE

SERVES 4

Preparation time: 20 minutes
Kcal per serving: 120
P = 1g, F = 12g, C = 1g

½ cup meat or fish broth
1 shallot, peeled and finely
chopped
⅔ cup heavy cream
1 tbsp butter
2 tbsps chopped fresh dill
1 tsp lemon juice
salt
freshly ground white pepper

1. Heat the broth in a pan, add the shallot, and boil the liquid over a high heat until it has reduced by half.
2. Add half the cream, bring back to the boil, and allow to reduce. Remove the pan from the heat. Stir in the butter, a little at a time, making sure each piece has been

Carefully fold the whipped dill cream into the sauce using an egg whisk.

fully incorporated before adding any more.
3. Whip the remaining cream until stiff. Fold the dill into the cream, and then fold the mixture into the sauce. Stir in the lemon juice, and season to taste with salt and pepper. Serve with poached or steamed fish, beef, or lamb.

NEW MUSTARD SAUCE

SERVES 4

Preparation time: 15 minutes
Kcal per serving: 325
P = 2g, F = 35g, C = 1g

⅔ cup butter
2 tbsps water
2 egg yolks
juice of 1 lemon
salt
freshly ground white pepper
1 tbsp French mustard
1 tbsp fresh tarragon leaves

1. Melt 1 tbsp of the butter in a small, heavy-based pan. Pour in the water and beat thoroughly with an egg whisk. Remove from the heat, and beat in the egg yolks.
2. Return the pan to a low heat. Gradually beat in the remaining butter, a little at a time, making sure that each piece has been fully incor-

Stir the mustard into the sauce and add the tarragon leaves.

porated before adding more. Do not allow the sauce to boil. Stir in the lemon juice, and season to taste with salt and pepper.
3. Remove the sauce from the heat, and stir in the mustard and tarragon. This sauce goes perfectly with fish, meat, or poached eggs.

Dishes from Around the World

*T*his chapter is truly a world-wide expedition, exploring the soups of China, sampling the cuisine of Russia, the Balkans, and Ireland, and lingering for a little longer in France and Italy. A culinary journey through soups and stews promises interesting new flavors, unfamiliar aromas – and both down-to-earth fare and sophisticated feasts. It is well worth trying and tasting a few new recipes, such as Italian Minestrone. Hot, spicy food is represented by the Mexican Chili con Carne or the Hungarian Goulash Soup, while French Vegetable Purée Soup or fine Avocado and Sherry Cream Soup tempt with their delicate flavors. Sauces from around the world are a perfect addition to the cook's repertoire.

Creole Vegetable Stew with Okra (recipe page 54)

ITALIAN MINESTRONE
Minestrone di verdura

SERVES 4 ■ ■
Preparation time: about 3 hours
Soaking time: overnight
Kcal per serving: 665
P = 25g, F = 29g, C = 76g

⅔ cup Great Northern or red
    kidney beans
4 slices smoked streaky
    bacon, or lean belly of
    pork
2 sticks of celery
2 carrots
3 Idaho potatoes
1 onion
2 small zucchini
2 cups tomatoes
1 garlic clove
¼ head of Savoy cabbage
½ cup small green beans
1½ cups young peas or 1 bulb
    of fennel
4 tbsps olive oil
1 tbsp finely chopped fresh
    parsley
2 tsps torn fresh basil leaves
1 tsp chopped fresh sage
2½ quarts water
6 ounces (¾ cup) spaghetti,
    macaroni, or rice
salt
4 tbsps freshly grated
    Parmesan cheese

1. Place the dried beans in a bowl and cover with cold water. Set aside overnight to soak. The following day, drain the beans, and transfer them to a pan. Cover with water, bring to the boil, lower the heat and simmer gently for 1½-2½ hours, until tender. Drain and set aside.
2. Dice the bacon or pork. Wash the celery and cut into matchstick strips. Peel the carrots and cut into matchstick strips. Peel and dice the potatoes and onion. Wash and dice the zucchini. Blanch, peel, seed, and chop the tomatoes. Peel and finely chop the garlic. Wash and shred the cabbage. Wash the green beans and break each into two or three

Soak the beans overnight in cold water.

Carrots, green beans, tomatoes, zucchini, celery, and garlic are important ingredients in minestrone.

pieces. Shell the peas or cut the fennel into fine strips.
3. Heat the oil in a saucepan, and gently fry the bacon, onions, garlic, and parsley. Add the basil and sage, and fry for 5 minutes. Add the celery, carrots, zucchini, potatoes, and fennel, if using. Pour over the water, and season with salt. Add the cooked beans, cover, and cook for 1½ hours.
4. Add the tomatoes and green beans, and cook for a further 30 minutes. Add the pasta or rice and the peas, and cook for a further 20 minutes. Season the soup with salt. Serve in individual soup bowls and garnish with grated Parmesan cheese.

FRENCH VEGETABLE PURÉE SOUP
Potage crème de légumes

SERVES 4 ■
Preparation time: 50 minutes
Kcal per serving: 320
P = 7g, F = 23g, C = 21g

3 carrots
3 potatoes
1 young kohlrabi
2 leeks
½ cup butter
1 sprig celery leaves
1½ quarts meat broth
⅔ cup shelled young peas
2 tbsps chopped fresh chervil

1. Peel the carrots, potatoes, and kohlrabi, and chop into large cubes or cut into strips. Trim and wash the leeks and cut into strips. Melt 2 tbsps of the butter in a pan, and gently fry the vegetables for 5 minutes.
2. Add the celery leaves and the broth, bring to the boil, and cook for 30 minutes. Add the peas, and cook for a further 10 minutes.
3. Rub the soup through a sieve, or purée it using a hand-held mixer. Gently stir in the remaining butter, one piece at a time, making sure each piece is fully incorporated before adding the next. Garnish the soup with finely chopped chervil, and serve immediately.

> **TIP**
>
> *If the kohlrabi has any tender leaves, chop them and use in the soup. Frozen peas may be used instead of fresh ones.*

LEEK AND POTATO SOUP
Potage aux poireaux et aux pommes de terre

SERVES 4 ■
Preparation time: 1 hour
Kcal per serving: 310
P = 6g, F = 22g, C = 22g

4 leeks
5 potatoes
4 tbsps butter
1½ quarts meat broth
½ cup heavy cream
salt
freshly ground white pepper

1. Wash the leeks and cut into ¾-inch slices. Peel and dice the potatoes.
2. Melt the butter in a pan, and gently fry the leeks until transparent. Add the potatoes, and fry for a further 3 minutes, stirring constantly. Add the broth, bring to the boil and cook for 40 minutes.
3. Rub the soup through a sieve or purée it with a small amount of liquid in a food processor. Make sure that the leeks are fully incorporated into the purée.

> **TIP**
>
> *Adding fresh sorrel, cut into strips and gently fried in butter, makes a Potage Santé – another excellent soup.*

4. Return the soup to the pan, stir in the cream, and bring to the boil. Season generously, and serve immediately.
Accompaniment: toasted French bread.

PROVENÇAL FISH SOUP
Soupe de poisson à la provençale

SERVES 6 ■■
Preparation time: 1¼ hours
Kcal per serving: 375
P = 23g, F = 25g, C = 13g

2½ pounds white fish (e.g.
*   porgy, tilefish, weakfish,*
*   red snapper, grouper,*
*   mullet), cleaned*
2 large fish heads
4 soft-shelled crabs or ½ cup
*   bay shrimp*
4 garlic cloves
2 leeks
1 carrot
2 onions
2 tomatoes
½ cup olive oil
1 tbsp tomato paste
2 quarts water
1 bayleaf
2 thyme sprigs
4 dried fennel sprigs
3 parsley sprigs
sea salt
cayenne pepper
½ tsp saffron threads
strip of orange rind
½ French stick
1 tbsp freshly grated Swiss
*   cheese*

1. Wash the fish and pat dry.
2. Remove the eyes from the fish heads with a pointed knife. Remove and discard the gills. Wash the crabs or shrimp under running water. Crush them in a food processor or use a pestle and mortar.
3. Crush 3 of the garlic cloves, unpeeled, using a pestle and mortar or a garlic press. Wash the leeks, and peel the carrot and onions. Cut them into strips. Quarter the tomatoes.
4. Heat the oil in a large skillet, and stir-fry the leeks, carrot and onions for a few minutes. Add the fish, fish heads, and the crab or shrimp paste, and fry for a further 5 minutes. Add the tomatoes, tomato paste and water. Tie the herbs together

to make a bouquet garni and add to the pan. Season to taste with sea salt and cayenne pepper, and add the saffron and orange rind. Bring to the boil and cook over a high heat for 15 minutes.
5. Remove and discard the fish heads, orange rind, and bouquet garni. Purée the fish and vegetables in a food processor, then rub the purée through a sieve to remove any remaining bones. Return the soup to the pan, and cook for a further 30 minutes.
6. Slice the French stick thinly and place it in a hot oven to dry, rather than toast it. Cut the remaining garlic clove in half and rub it over the bread. Place the slices of flavored bread in 6 soup bowls, and pour the soup over them. Sprinkle with grated cheese and serve immediately.
Recommended wine: a rosé from Provence.

> ### TIP
> *If liked, the bread slices may also be coated with rouille (saffron-colored mayonnaise) or aïoli (garlic mayonnaise), in which case omit the grated cheese.*

Several different varieties of fish are required to make Provençal Fish Soup.

Cook the fried vegetables, fish, herbs, and spices over a high heat.

Purée the mixture after removing the fish heads.

Rub the fish and vegetable purée through a sieve to remove any remaining bones

HUNGARIAN GOULASH SOUP
Bogrács Gulyás

SERVES 4 ■
Preparation time: 2 hours
Kcal per serving: 270
P = 23g, F = 14g, C = 12g

14 ounces steak
2 onions
1 garlic clove
4 tbsps beef fat or lard
1 tbsp sweet paprika or 1 tsp
*   strong paprika*
5 cups water
salt
1 tbsp tomato paste
3 large potatoes

1. Wash the steak and pat dry. Cut it into small chunks. Peel and dice the onions. Peel the garlic.
2. Melt the beef fat or lard in a heavy-based pan, and fry the onions for 5-7 minutes until transparent. Sprinkle with the paprika and immediately add the meat and garlic. Fry, stirring frequently, for 15 minutes until the meat juice has evaporated. Pour over a little water, season with salt and stir in the tomato purée. Cook the goulash until all the liquid has again evaporated. Add about half the remaining water and braise over a very low heat for just under 2 hours. (The meat should braise rather than boil in the minimum amount of liquid.)
3. Peel the potatoes and chop into large cubes. Cook them in lightly salted boiling water for 15 minutes or until nearly tender. Drain. Add the remaining water to the goulash and bring to the boil. Add the parboiled potatoes, and boil for a further 15 minutes until the potatoes are just starting to disintegrate. Add a little more salt, if necessary, and serve immediately. If liked, the goulash soup can also be flavored with a little marjoram and caraway seeds.

ITALIAN CREAM OF TOMATO SOUP

ITALIAN CREAM OF TOMATO SOUP

Crema di pomodori

SERVES 4 ▪

Preparation time: 30 minutes
Kcal per serving: 260
P = 4g, F = 20g, C = 17g

2½ pounds tomatoes
1 small onion
1 garlic clove
2 cups meat broth
1 tsp sugar
1 clove
1 rosemary sprig
salt
freshly ground black pepper
½ cup heavy cream
1 tbsp torn basil leaves
2 thick slices white bread,
 crusts removed
2 tbsps butter
2 tbsps freshly grated
 Parmesan cheese

1. Wash and chop the tomatoes. Peel and chop the onion. Peel the garlic. Place the tomatoes in a pan and add enough broth to cover. Add the sugar, onion, garlic, clove, and rosemary, and season to taste with salt. Bring the mixture to the boil, and cook until the tomatoes are completely soft. Rub the soup through a sieve, return it to the pan and cook for a further 3 minutes.
2. Beat a little of the soup into the cream with a whisk. Beat the cream mixture into the rest of the soup. Bring the soup back to the boil, stirring constantly. Stir in the basil.
3. Dice the bread. Melt the butter in a pan, and fry the bread cubes until golden-brown.
4. Season the soup to taste with salt and pepper. Pour into soup bowls, add the croûtons (bread cubes), and serve immediately. Hand the grated cheese separately.

Rub the aromatic tomato broth through a fine sieve using a wooden spoon.

Stir the heavy cream into the tomato soup.

Fry cubes of bread in hot butter until golden-brown, stirring them constantly so that they do not burn.

Use freshly grated Parmesan for sprinkling over the soup.

GREEK CHICKEN AND RICE SOUP

Suppa avgolemono

SERVES 4 ▪

Preparation time: 15 minutes
Kcal per serving: 190
P = 7g, F = 7g, C = 25g

1½ quarts chicken broth
salt
½ cup long-grain rice
1 tbsp cornstarch
⅓ cup milk
3 egg yolks
1 tsp chopped fresh parsley
juice of 1 lemon

1. Season the broth with a little salt, and bring to the boil in a large pan. Rinse the rice in cold water and add to the broth. Bring back to the boil and cook for 12 minutes.
2. Thoroughly mix together the cornstarch, milk, and egg yolk in a bain-marie or heatproof bowl set over a pan of hot water. Gradually beat in the broth with a whisk. Bring the soup just to the boil, but do not allow it to boil vigorously. Leave it to simmer for a few minutes.
3. Stir in the parsley and lemon juice, making sure the soup does not curdle.

> ## TIP
> *In Greece, the same recipe is used to prepare another delicious soup using fat-free lamb broth.*

AVOCADO AND SHERRY CREAM SOUP

SERVES 4 ▪

Preparation time: 20 minutes
Kcal per serving: 385
P = 4g, F = 40g, C = 3g

2 avocados
juice of ½ lemon
3 cups chicken broth
½ cup sour cream
⅓ cup dry sherry
salt
freshly ground white pepper

1. Cut the avocados in half lengthwise and pit them. Peel the flesh and sprinkle it with lemon juice. Cut 3 of the avocado halves into pieces. Cover the remaining half and set it aside.
2. Heat the chicken broth. Purée the avocado pieces with the hot broth and sour cream.
3. Pour the soup into a pan and bring it to the boil, beating constantly with a whisk. Stir in the sherry, and remove the soup from the heat. Season to taste with salt and pepper.
4. Finely dice the remaining avocado half, and stir it into the soup. Serve immediately.

> ## TIP
> *Avocado and Sherry Soup also tastes delicious chilled, in which case the chicken broth must first be skimmed of all fat.*

CHILI CON CARNE WITH BEANS

SERVES 4
Preparation time: 3 hours
Soaking time: overnight
Kcal per serving: 460
P = 39g, F = 18g, C = 36g

1 cup red kidney beans
1 quart water
3 onions
2 tbsps oil
14 ounces ground beef
1-4 small dried red chilies
   (chile arbol or chile peqin)
1¼ cups chicken broth
1¾ cups canned tomatoes (or
   green tomatoes, if
   available)
1 red pepper
2 garlic cloves
½ tsp dried oregano
½ tsp ground cumin
½ tsp salt
½ tsp chili powder

Halve the red pepper, cut out the stem and seeds, and slice into strips.

Chop two peeled garlic cloves and add them to the ground meat.

Recommended drink: red table wine, beer, or tequila.

TIP

This dish is hot and spicy – a single chili is sufficient for more sensitive palates. Chili con Carne may also be served in baked taco shells. Accompany with bowls of green salad, sour cream, salsa, and hot, frsh corn or wheat tortillas..

1. Place the beans in a bowl, add the water and set aside overnight to soak. The following day, transfer the beans and their soaking water to a pan, bring to the boil, and boil vigorously for 15 minutes. Lower the heat and cook for 1½-2 hours until they are almost soft.
2. Meanwhile, peel and dice the onions. Heat the oil in a pan, and fry the beef and onions for 5-8 minutes.
3. Cut the dried chilies into strips. Place them in a bowl, add the chicken broth and set aside to soak.
4. Drain and chop the tomatoes. Stir the tomatoes into the ground beef. Wash and seed the pepper and cut into strips. Peel and finely dice the garlic. Stir the chilies, pepper, garlic, oregano, cumin, salt, chilli powder, and chicken broth into the beef mixture. Cook in an uncovered pan over a low heat for about 2 hours. Drain the kidney beans, stir into the chili con carne and simmer for a further 30 minutes.

POT-AU-FEU

SERVES 8-10 ■ ■
Preparation time: 4½ hours
Kcal per serving, serving 8: 680
P = 51g, F = 33g, C = 35g

1¾ pounds shin of beef
2 beef bones
4 quarts water
¼ tsp peppercorns
1 thyme sprig
1 bayleaf
3 parsley sprigs
2 onions
2 cloves
1 tomato
1 garlic clove
1 tbsp sea salt
2½ pounds beef brisket
1 large chicken
4 leeks
6 large carrots or 3 carrots
   and 3 turnips
½ head celery
1 small Savoy cabbage
6 potatoes
3 marrow bones (each cut
   into 3 pieces)
8-10 thin slices of white
   bread, crusts removed

1. Wash the beef and the bones and place in a Dutch oven. Add the water, peppercorns, and herbs.
2. Roast an unpeeled onion in a preheated oven at 400°F until the peel is dark brown. Peel the remaining onion and stud it with the cloves. Place the onions, tomatoes, and unpeeled garlic clove in the pan and bring the mixture to the boil.
3. Skim off the froth. When no more froth builds up, season with salt, add the brisket, and partially cover the pan. Cook for 2 hours. Then add the chicken, partially cover, and cook for 1 hour.
4. Trim and wash the leeks and tie them together with cotton thread. Peel and coarsely chop the carrots and turnips, if using. Trim, wash, and coarsely chop the celery. Add the vegetables to the soup.

5. Transfer a little broth containing most of the fat to a second pan. Remove the outer leaves of the Savoy cabbage and cut out the stem. Cook the cabbage in the broth for about 30 minutes. Peel and halve the potatoes. Transfer a little more broth to a separate pan and cook the potatoes for about 20 minutes.
6. Wrap the marrow bones in cheesecloth and add them to the broth for the last 20 minutes of cooking time. Remove the meat and vegetables with a slotted spoon and keep warm. Strain the broth and skim off the fat. Return to the pan and boil to reduce the liquid.
7. The pot-au-feu is served as two courses:
– Toast the appropriate number of bread slices. While still hot, spread them with marrow from the marrow bones and sprinkle with sea salt. Serve together with the hot soup.
– Slice the beef and cut the chicken into portions. Place the meat on a large, heated plate and arrange the vegetables around the meat.
Recommended wine: a young Beaujolais.

CREOLE VEGETABLE STEW WITH OKRA

Gombos à la créole
(photograph page 44/45)

SERVES 4
*Preparation time: 1½ hours
Kcal per serving: 435
P = 17g, F = 16g, C = 56g*

4 cups young, fresh okra
2 onions
2-3 garlic cloves
3 beefsteak tomatoes
4 tbsps olive oil or peanut oil
1 tsp coriander (cilantro)
    seeds
salt
freshly ground black pepper
juice of ½ lemon
1 cup long-grain rice
¼ tsp saffron
1 clove
1 cup raw shrimp
2 tbsps butter

Fry the onion, garlic, okra, and tomatoes in oil.

Mix the vegetables well after seasoning, cover with a lid and braise for 1 hour.

Shell the shrimp and toss them in butter. Then combine them with the rice and vegetables.

1. Trim, wash, and dry the okra. Peel and dice the onions. Peel and thinly slice the garlic. Blanch, skin, and dice the tomatoes.
2. Heat the oil, and fry the onions and garlic until transparent. Sprinkle with the coriander (cilantro) and stir-fry for a further 2-3 minutes.
3. Add the okra, and fry until it starts to soften. Stir in the tomatoes, and season to taste with salt and pepper. Cover the pan, reduce the heat, and braise the vegetables for 1 hour until soft. Add the lemon juice.
4. Meanwhile, cook the rice for 20 minutes in plenty of lightly salted boiling water containing the saffron and clove. Drain.
5. Shell the shrimp. Melt the butter, add the shrimp and toss them briefly in the butter until colored.
6. Combine the rice, okra, and shrimp in a large pan, cover with a lid, and leave to stand for 5 minutes to allow the flavors to mingle. Serve hot.

> **TIP**
>
> *Canned okra is also available, but young, fresh okra tastes better.*

BÉARNAISE STEW

Garbure béarnaise

SERVES 4 ■ ■
*Preparation time: 3 hours
Kcal per serving: 540
P = 50g, F = 19g, C = 42g*

2 goose legs
2 quarts water
salt
freshly ground black pepper
4 large carrots
4 potatoes
1 head of celery
1 large white cabbage
2 leeks
1 large onion
4 slices of toast
4 tbsps freshly grated Swiss
    cheese
4 tbsps butter, melted

1. Wash the goose legs. Place them in a pan with the water and a pinch of salt. Bring to the boil and simmer for 1½ hours.
2. Peel the carrots and potatoes. Trim and wash the celery and cabbage. Coarsely grate the carrots, potatoes, and celery. Shred the cabbage. Trim, wash, and thinly slice the leeks. Peel and thinly slice the onion.
3. Add the vegetables to the pan, and cook for a further 1 hour. Remove the goose legs from the broth and set aside. Rub the vegetables through a sieve, or purée them with a hand-held mixer. Remove the goose meat from the bones, chop finely, and add it to the vegetable purée.
4. Transfer the stew to an ovenproof dish and arrange the slices of toast on top. Sprinkle over the cheese and pour over the melted butter. Bake in a preheated oven at 475°F until golden brown and crusty on top. Serve immediately straight from the dish.

IRISH STEW

SERVES 4 ■
*Preparation time: 2 hours
Kcal per serving: 455
P = 28g, F = 23g, C = 34g*

About 2 pounds lean stewing
    lamb
2½ pounds potatoes
6 large onions
salt
freshly ground black pepper
1 bayleaf
2 cups meat broth or water
1 tbsp butter

1. Wash the meat and pat dry. Cut into chunks, if necessary. Peel and slice the potatoes and onions.
2. Place half the potato slices in the base of a large pan, cover with the sliced onion, and then with the meat. Season generously with salt and pepper, and top with the remaining potato slices. Season once more, add the bayleaf and add the meat broth or water.
3. Grease one side of a sheet of aluminum foil or parchment paper with the butter and place it over the stew. Cover the pan tightly with a lid, and braise slowly over a medium heat for about 1½ hours. Serve in deep plates.

> **TIP**
>
> *An authentic Irish stew does not contain cabbage, although it is often included in recipes.*

MALTESE SAUCE

(photograph page 27)

SERVES 4 ■■
*Preparation time: 25 minutes
Kcal per serving: 320
P = 2g, F = 34g, C = 1g*

2 tbsps water
1 tbsp white wine vinegar
½ tsp salt
rind of ½ blood orange, cut
    into strips
2 egg yolks
2 tbsps blood orange juice
pinch of sugar
⅔ cup butter
pinch of cayenne pepper

*Stir the reduced orange vinegar
into the frothy egg yolk and
orange juice cream.*

1. Bring the water and vinegar to the boil in a small pan. Add the salt and orange rind, and boil until only 1 tbsp of liquid remains. Remove from the heat and set aside to cool.
2. Beat together the egg yolks, orange juice, and sugar in a bain marie or heatproof bowl set over a pan of hot water until frothy. Beat in the reduced orange vinegar.
3. Continue to beat the sauce until it is thick and creamy.
4. Dice the butter. Beat the butter into the sauce one piece at a time, making sure each piece is incorporated before adding the next. Season lightly with cayenne pepper. Serve with fish, duck, asparagus, or oyster plant.

BULGARIAN CHILLED YOGURT SOUP

Tarator

SERVES 4 ■
*Preparation time: 15 minutes
Kcal per serving: 245
P = 7g, F = 20g, C = 9g*

2 cups yogurt
1 cup iced water
1 tbsp white wine vinegar
2 garlic cloves
salt
freshly ground white pepper
3 tbsps olive oil
1 tbsp chopped dill
1 cucumber
1 tbsp chopped walnuts
1 dill sprig

1. Beat together the yogurt, water, and vinegar. Peel and crush the garlic with a little salt with a pestle and mortar or mince it. Gradually combine the garlic with the oil. Beat the yogurt mixture with the oil, stir in the chopped dill, and season with pepper.
2. Wash and grate or thinly slice the cucumber. Stir it into the chilled soup. Sprinkle with the chopped nuts and garnish with dill.

TIP

Adding sour cream to this soup makes it even tastier. Fresh mint may also be used instead of dill

---

GREEN HERB SAUCE

Salsa verde

SERVES 4 ■
*Preparation time: 20 minutes
Kcal per serving: 295
P = 1g, F = 31g, C = 3g*

1 bunch parsley
4 basil sprigs
1 garlic clove
2 tbsps capers
2 anchovy fillets
2 tbsps breadcrumbs
2 tbsps white wine vinegar
salt
freshly ground black pepper
½ cup olive oil

*Finely chop the parsley, basil,
capers, and anchovies before
combining them with the
breadcrumb mixture.*

1. Remove the parsley and basil leaves from their stems. Peel the garlic. Finely chop together the parsley, basil, garlic, capers, and anchovies. Combine the breadcrumbs and vinegar, and season to taste with salt. Mix together the breadcrumb and herb mixtures.
2. Gradually stir in the oil to make a thick sauce. Finally, season with freshly ground pepper. This sauce goes especially well with boiled meat and fish.

HOLLANDAISE SAUCE

SERVES 6 ■■
*Preparation time: 20 minutes
Kcal per serving: 350
P = 2g, F = 38g, C = 0g*

4 tbsps water
1 tbsp white wine vinegar
½ tsp salt
freshly ground white pepper
3 egg yolks
1 cup butter
pinch of freshly grated
    nutmeg

1. Place half the water and the vinegar in a small pan, season with salt and pepper, and bring to the boil. Boil until only 1 tsp liquid remains. Set aside to cool.
2. Place the egg yolks and remaining water in a bain-marie or heatproof bowl set over a pan of hot water and beat until frothy. Beat in the reduced vinegar, and continue beating until the mixture is thick and creamy.
3. Remove from the heat and continue beating the sauce, gradually adding the butter in small pieces at a time, ensuring that each piece is fully incorporated before adding the next. If required, season with a little more salt and add a pinch of nutmeg. If the sauce becomes too thick, beat in a few drops of lukewarm water. Serve with artichokes, asparagus, or fish.

FRENCH MUSTARD SAUCE
Sauce diable

SERVES 4 ■
Preparation time: 15 minutes
Kcal per serving: 320
P = 2g, F = 34g, C = 1g

⅔ cup chilled butter
1 tbsp water
2 egg yolks
juice of ½ lemon
salt
freshly ground black pepper
1 tsp French mustard
1 tbsp chopped fresh
*   tarragon*

1. Melt 1 tbsp of the butter in a small pan. Beat in the water, using an egg whisk. Remove the pan from the heat and beat in the egg yolks.
2. Return the pan to a low heat and beat in the remaining butter in small pieces at a time, making sure that each piece is fully incorporated before adding the next. Do not allow the sauce to boil.
3. Add the lemon juice, and season to taste with salt and pepper. Remove the pan from the heat and stir in the mustard and tarragon. Serve with poached fish, boiled meats or egg dishes.

> **TIP**
> *If the sauce curdles, beat in 1-2 tbsps water.*

MAYONNAISE PROVENÇALE
Rouille
(photograph page 29)

SERVES 4 ■
Preparation time: 10 minutes
Kcal per serving: 320
P = 1g, F = 31g, C = 8g

4 tbsps breadcrumbs or 1
*   cold, boiled potato*
4 tbsps fish broth (if using
*   breadcrumbs)*
2 garlic cloves
1 small red chili
¼ tsp salt
pinch of saffron threads,
*   crushed*
8 tbsps olive oil

The small red chili can be easily crushed using a pestle and mortar.

1. Place the breadcrumbs in a bowl and add the fish broth, if using, and set aside to soak. Peel and mash the potato, if using. Peel the garlic and seed the chili. Purée both in a blender or food processor, then add the soaked breadcrumbs or the potato, salt, and saffron.
2. With the blender or food processor still running, add the olive oil, a drop at a time at first, and then in a thin stream. The finished mayonnaise should be thick and smooth. Use as an accompaniment to fish soups, especially bouillabaisse and other fish soups from Provence. This mayonnaise is also delicious on toasted French bread slices.

GARLIC MAYONNAISE
Aïoli

SERVES 4 ■
Preparation time: 10 minutes
Kcal per serving: 455
P = 1g, F = 50g, C = 0g

4 garlic cloves
1 egg yolk
¼ tsp salt
1 tbsp lemon juice
¾ cup extra virgin olive oil

1. Peel the garlic and purée in a blender or food processor. Add the egg yolk, salt, and lemon juice, and combine thoroughly.
2. With the blender or food processor still running, add the olive oil, drop by drop at first, and then in a thin stream. The finished mayonnaise should be thick and smooth. Use as an accompaniment to fish soups, fish dishes, especially salt cod, and with boiled vegetables.

> **TIP**
> *A good wine vinegar may be used to make the aïoli instead of lemon juice.*

SORREL SAUCE
Sauce à l'oseille

SERVES 4 ■
Preparation time: 30 minutes
Kcal per serving: 260
P = 2g, F = 24g, C = 3g

3 ounces sorrel
2 shallots
1 cup meat or fish broth
5 tbsps white wine
4 tbsps dry vermouth
⅔ cup sour cream
3 tbsps butter, diced
juice of ½ lemon
salt
freshly ground white pepper

1. Wash the sorrel, cut off the stalks, cut out the thick main stems, and shred the larger leaves. Drain well. Peel and dice the shallots.
2. Pour the broth into a skillet and add the wine, vermouth, and shallots. Boil over a high heat until the liquid develops a syrupy consistency.
3. Add the sour cream, and continue to boil until the sauce is thick. Stir in the sorrel and boil for 30 seconds.
4. Remove the sauce from the heat and stir in the butter, one piece at a time. Add the lemon juice, and season to taste with salt and pepper. Sorrel sauce goes well with boiled and steamed fish, and tastes especially good with salmon.

Cooking for Special Occasions

*T*he recipes in this section prove that soups and stews can be delicious as well as satisfying. The following dishes are not intended to be filling, but are subtly flavored and served either as appetizers or entrées for those with light appetites. Even lentil soups, generally central to plain home cooking, are transformed into first-class meals; soups made with fish and seafood make gourmet dishes for festive occasions, and what is more, this chapter contains a treasure trove of ideas for sauces, from classics to new creations, ideal for combining with fish, meats and vegetables.

Fish Soup with Potatoes and Shrimp (recipe page 64)

CLEAR OXTAIL SOUP WITH VEGETABLES

SERVES 8 ■ ■ ■

Preparation time: 4 hours 20 minutes
Kcal per portion: 355
P = 37g, F = 19g, C = 7g

FOR CLARIFYING:
½ cup carrots, peeled and diced
½ cup celery, diced
½ cup leeks, diced
10 ounces beef, chopped into fairly large pieces
3 egg whites, whisked
1 cup water

FOR THE SOUP:
2 tbsps clarified butter
2½ pounds oxtail, chopped
2 onions, peeled and thickly sliced
4 carrots, peeled and diced
4 sticks celery or ½ celery root, diced
4 leeks, diced
salt
freshly ground black pepper
2 tomatoes, skinned and finely chopped
pinch of sugar
1 small thyme sprig
1 small bayleaf
1¼ cups red wine
2 quarts meat broth
2 tbsps Madeira
1 tbsp whisky (optional)
2 tbsps snipped fresh chives

FOR THE GARNISH:
1 carrot, peeled and thinly sliced
1 turnip, thinly sliced

1. First prepare the clarifying mixture by combining the diced vegetables, beef, whisked egg white, and water. Place the mixture in the refrigerator until it is required.
2. To make the soup, melt the clarified butter over a high heat, and fry the pieces of oxtail on all sides. Add the onions, diced carrots, celery or celery root, and leeks. Season to taste with salt and pepper, and fry until the onions are transparent and

the other vegetables are light brown. Add the tomatoes, sugar, thyme, and bayleaf, reduce the heat, cover, and braise for 30 minutes.
3. Meanwhile, make the garnish. Using a small cookie cutter, cut out small stars or other decorative shapes from the carrot and turnip slices. Cook them in lightly salted boiling water until tender but still firm to the bite. Drain and set aside.
4. Add the red wine to the braised vegetables, and boil over a high heat until the liquid has reduced by half. Add the broth, lower the heat, and simmer for about 2½ hours or until the oxtail is very tender. From time to time, top up with water to replace the liquid that has evaporated. Remove the soup from the heat and set aside to cool.
5. When the soup is cold, strain it into a clean pan. Set the vegetables and meat aside.
6. To clarify the soup, add the prepared clarifying mixture and bring to the boil, stirring constantly. Lower the heat and simmer gently for 30 minutes.
7. Meanwhile, remove the oxtail meat from the bones and dice it finely.
8. Strain the soup through cheesecloth into a pan. Heat through once more, season to taste with salt, pepper, and stir in the Madeira and whisky, if using. Divide the vegetables, diced meats and chives between 8 heated soup bowls, pour over the soup and garnish with the vegetable stars. Serve immediately.
Accompaniment: cheese puffs.
Recommended wine: a white or red Bordeaux.

Prepare the clarifying mixture with the diced vegetables, meat, egg white, and water.

Using small cookie cutters, cut out decorative shapes from the turnip and carrot slices.

To clarify the soup, add the prepared mixture to the cold broth.

Remove the cooked oxtail meat from the bone and chop finely.

CREAM OF POTATO SOUP WITH CHICKEN LIVERS

SERVES 4 ■ ■

Preparation time: 50 minutes
Kcal per portion: 405
P = 14g, F = 32g, C = 16g

1 tbsp butter
1 onion, peeled and finely chopped
14 ounces potatoes, peeled
1 quart meat broth
2 slices bacon, rind removed
1 cup heavy cream
salt
freshly ground black pepper
⅔ cup chicken livers
1 tbsp clarified butter
1 tbsp chopped fresh marjoram
2 tbsps cress or a few marjoram leaves (optional)

1. Melt the butter in a pan, and lightly fry the onion until transparent.
2. Add the potatoes and the broth, bring to the boil and simmer for about 20 minutes.
3. Finely dice the bacon, and dry-fry until crisp. Remove from the pan with a slotted spoon and set aside on absorbent paper.
4. Purée the soup in a blender or with a hand-held mixer. Return it to the pan and stir in ½ cup of the cream. Bring to the boil, and season to taste with salt and pepper. Whip the remaining cream until it forms stiff peaks, then add it to the soup.
5. Cut the chicken livers crosswise into strips. Melt the clarified butter, and fry the chicken livers over a high heat.
6. Divide the bacon and chopped marjoram between 4 heated soup plates or bowls, and pour the soup over. Arrange the livers on top and garnish with cress or marjoram leaves, if using.
Accompaniment: bread.
Recommended wine: red table wine.

CLEAR OXTAIL SOUP
WITH VEGETABLES

CREAM OF CHICKEN SOUP WITH JUMBO SHRIMP

SERVES 6

Preparation time: 1½ hours
Kcal per portion: 655
P = 40g, F = 52g, C = 7g

1 chicken
1 carrot
1 leek
1 stick of celery
salt
freshly ground white pepper
2 cucumbers
1 onion
2 tbsps butter
2 tbsps all-purpose flour
⅔ cup heavy cream
pinch of freshly grated
    nutmeg
½ cup jumbo shrimp, shelled
    and deveined
1 tbsp chopped dill
6 dill sprigs

1. Place the chicken in a large pan and cover with cold water. Bring to the boil over high heat; drain. Add fresh cold water, bring to the boil, and cook the chicken for 30 minutes.
2. Meanwhile, peel and dice the carrot. Trim, wash, and dice the leek. Trim, wash, and dice the celery. Add the carrot, leek, and celery to the broth, season with a little salt and simmer over a low heat for a further 1 hour, occasionally skimming off any froth from the surface of the liquid.

> **TIP**
>
> *The chicken can be eaten as an entrée, in, for example, a chicken salad.*

3. Strain the broth and use the chicken in another dish.
4. Peel and chop the cucumbers. Peel and chop the onion.

Add finely diced carrots, leeks and celery to the stock, and simmer for a further 1 hour.

5. Melt 1 tbsp of the butter, and fry the onion until transparent. Add the cucumber and gently fry. Add ¾ cup of the broth and bring to the boil.
6. Heat 2 tbsps of the remaining butter, add the flour and cook, stirring constantly, for 1-2 minutes, without allowing it to brown. Remove the pan from the heat, and stir in 2 cups of hot, but not boiling broth. Stir until the liquid is smooth. Return the pan to a low heat, and simmer for 20-25 minutes.
7. Purée the soup, together with the cucumber and onion mixture, in a blender or food processor. Add the cream and beat in the remaining butter with a whisk. Season with salt, pepper, and nutmeg. Cut the jumbo shrimp crosswise into small pieces. Add the shrimp to the soup, and heat through briefly.
8. Transfer to soup bowls or plates, sprinkle with the chopped dill, and garnish each bowl with a dill sprig, if liked.
Accompaniment: French bread.
Recommended wine: dry white wine.

FISH SOUP WITH POTATOES AND SHRIMP

(photograph page 60/61)

SERVES 4

Preparation time: 40 minutes
Kcal per portion: 325
P = 23g, F = 19g, C = 8g

2 potatoes
1¼ pounds monkfish or cod
    fillets
2 ounces smoked, lean
    bacon, rind removed and
    diced
1 large onion, peeled and
    chopped
1¼ pounds sole bones
1 quart hot water
salt
freshly ground black pepper
1 bayleaf
½ cup heavy cream
⅓ cup peeled cooked bay
    shrimp[
3 tbsps snipped, fresh chives

1. Peel and dice the potatoes. Cut the fish into 1-inch pieces.
2. Dry-fry the bacon until crisp. Add the onion, and fry until transparent.
3. Add the fish bones and the water, and bring to the boil. Skim off the froth, season to taste with salt and pepper, and add the bayleaf.
4. Cover and simmer over a low heat for about 15 minutes. Strain the broth into a clean pan, and return it to the heat.
5. Add the potatoes, and cook for about 15 minutes. Add the fish, and simmer for a further 5 minutes.
6. Add the cream and bay shrimp, and gently heat through. Season with more salt and pepper, if required, and serve garnished with chives.
Recommended wine: dry white wine.

CREAM OF ONION SOUP

SERVES 4

Preparation time: 45 minutes
Kcal per portion: 225
P = 4g, F = 15g, C = 16g

4 large onions
2 tbsps butter
2 tbsps all-purpose flour
2 tbsps white wine
3¼ cups meat broth
½ cup heavy cream
salt
freshly ground black pepper
pinch of cayenne pepper
1 tbsp finely chopped parsley
pinch of paprika

1. Peel and chop the onions. Melt the butter, and then gently fry the onions until transparent.
2. Sprinkle with the flour, and stir in the white wine. Add the broth, bring to the boil, and cook for about 30 minutes. Add 6 tbsps of the cream, and bring back to the boil. Season to taste with salt and pepper and add the cayenne pepper. Beat the remaining cream until stiff.
3. Pour the soup into heated plates or bowls, place a spoonful of cream in the center of each, sprinkle with a little paprika, and garnish with the parsley. Serve immediately.
Accompaniment: rye bread with butter.
Recommended drink: dry white wine.

> **TIP**
>
> *This soup is especially delicious if Bermuda or red onions are used; these are milder than ordinary cooking onions.*

RED PEPPER SOUP WITH SCALLOPS

SERVES 4 ■ ■ ■
Preparation time: 50 minutes
Kcal per portion: 210
P = 3g, F = 18g, C = 9g

4 scallops on the shell
2 tbsps olive oil
1 tbsp lemon juice
1 tsp chopped dill
salt
freshly ground white pepper
4 large red peppers
1 tbsp butter
2 tbsps finely chopped
    shallots
1 tbsp sugar
1 tbsp tomato paste
1 tbsp sweet paprika
juice of 1 lemon
1 cup chicken broth
½ cup heavy cream
1 rosemary sprig
1 parsley sprig
4 dill sprigs

Marinate the flesh of the scallops in the oil and lemon mixture for 2 hours.

Halve the peppers, remove the stems and seeds, and cut them into matchstick strips.

1. Open the scallops individually. Place one in a cloth, with the flat side of the shell facing upward. Run a large, pointed knife between the two halves of the shell and separate the scallop along the flat inner side. Raise the flat half of the shell, holding the other half firmly. Then run the knife along the edge of the flesh and carefully loosen it. Cut off the gray beard.
2. Remove the coral. Cut the flesh crosswise into very thin slices. Make a marinade by mixing together the olive oil, lemon juice, and chopped dill, and season with salt and pepper. Brush the marinade over the scallops, and set aside in the refrigerator for 1-2 hours.
3. Halve, seed, and wash the peppers. Slice them into matchstick strips.
4. Melt the butter in a pan, and gently fry the shallots for a few minutes. Sprinkle with the sugar, and cook, stirring constantly, until it begins to caramelize. Stir in the tomato purée, and add the peppers and the paprika. Add the lemon juice, chicken broth and cream. Bring to the boil, lower the heat, and simmer the mixture for 8-10 minutes. Add the rosemary and the parsley, and simmer gently for a further 2 minutes. Remove and discard the herbs.
5. Purée the soup in a blender or food processor and rub it through a sieve. Season to taste with salt and pepper, and pour it into bowls.
6. Season the scallops with salt and pepper, lay them on top of the soup, and garnish with dill.
Accompaniment: white bread.
Recommended wine: rosé.

CLAM CHOWDER

SERVES 6 ■ ■
Preparation time: 1 hour 10 minutes
Kcal per portion: 195
P = 10g, F = 12g, C = 9g

1 tbsp butter
2 tbsps chopped shallots
6 cups clams
½ cup white wine
2 cups chicken broth
1 small onion
2 leeks
1 tbsp vegetable oil
1 tbsp finely chopped lean
    bacon
1 small potato
2 cups hot milk
⅓ cup whipping cream
salt
freshly ground black pepper
pinch of freshly grated
    nutmeg
1 tbsp dry vermouth
2 tbsps snipped chives

Littleneck, geoduck, or soft shell clams may be used for this shellfish soup.

The shells will open during cooking. Discard any that remain closed.

Remove the clams from the shells and arrange on soup plates.

1. Melt the butter in a small pan, and gently fry the shallots until transparent. Scrub the clams under cold running water, and discard any that do not close when sharply tapped. Add the clams to the pan, and add the white wine. Bring to the boil, and cook until the shells open. Remove about one-third of the clams and set aside. Add the broth to the remaining clams, and cook for a further 30 minutes.
2. Peel and dice the onion. Trim, wash, and dice the leeks. Heat the oil, and gently fry the bacon, onion, and leeks until the vegetables are soft.
3. Peel and dice the potato. Transfer ½ cup of the clam broth to a clean pan, bring to the boil, and cook the potato until tender. Purée the onions, leek, bacon, and potato with a little broth, using a hand-held mixer. Pour in the hot milk and stir the mixture over the heat until it is almost boiling.
4. Drain the clams and add the juice to the soup.

Discard the clams. Whip the cream.
5. Remove the reserved clams from their shells and divide them between 6 soup plates. Season to taste with salt and pepper, and sprinkle with a little nutmeg and the vermouth. If the soup is too thick, dilute it with a little hot chicken broth. Pour the soup over the clams, top with swirls of cream, and serve garnished with chives.
Accompaniment: French stick.
Recommended wine: dry white wine.

PEA SOUP WITH MINT

SERVES 4 ■

Preparation time: 50 minutes
Kcal per portion: 205
P = 4g, F = 16g, C = 11g

4 tbsps butter
1 tbsp chopped onion
1 tbsp diced celery
1 tbsp chopped leek
1 tbsp all-purpose flour
2½ cups meat broth
salt
⅔ cup peas
⅔ cup heavy cream
2 slices white bread
½ tbsp chopped mint leaves

1. Melt 1 tbsp of the butter, and gently fry the onion, celery, and leek until soft. Sprinkle over the flour, and cook, stirring constantly for a further 2-3 minutes. Gradually stir in 2 cups of the broth. Bring to the boil, stirring constantly, lower the heat and simmer for 20-25 minutes. Season.
2. Bring the remaining broth to the boil, add the peas, and cook for about 8 minutes. Purée the peas in a blender and rub them through a sieve. Rub the soup through a sieve. Mix together the soup, pea purée, and the cream. Stir 1 tsp of the remaining butter into the soup, and briefly bring back to the boil.
3. Cut the bread into cubes. Melt the remaining butter, and fry the bread to make croûtons.

TIP

This soup can also be served chilled.

4. Serve the soup garnished with mint and hand the croûtons separately.
Accompaniment: coarse rye bread.
Recommended wine: red table wine.

CREAM OF LENTIL SOUP

SERVES 4 ■

Preparation time: 1 hour
Soaking time: overnight
Kcal per portion: 390
P = 23g, F = 17g, C = 37g

1 cup lentils
2 carrots
1 large onion
2 garlic cloves
2 tbsps butter
1 lean ham bone
1 sprig of celery leaves
1 bayleaf
1 tsp chopped fresh savory
1 quart meat broth
salt
freshly ground black pepper
4 ounces ham in one piece
2 slices white bread, crusts removed
¾ cup heavy cream
1 tbsp chopped fresh parsley (optional)

1. Wash the lentils, place in a bowl, cover them with boiled or bottled water, and leave to soak overnight.
2. Peel and slice the carrots. Peel and chop the onion. Peel and crush the garlic.
3. Melt 1 tbsp of the butter, and gently fry the onion until transparent.
4. Add the carrots, and fry for a further 5 minutes.
5. Add the lentils, together with their soaking water, the ham bone, celery leaves, bayleaf, savory, garlic, and meat broth.
6. Bring the mixture slowly to the boil, skimming off the froth as it forms. Partially cover the pan, and simmer over a low heat for about 15 minutes until the lentils are cooked. If globules of fat form on the surface of the soup, remove them with a spoon or absorbent paper. Set 2 ladles of lentils aside in a bowl.
7. Remove the ham bone, the bayleaf, and the celery leaves from the pan. Purée the soup with a hand-held mixer, and season to taste

Lentils come in a whole variety of sizes and colors. Most types should be soaked for about 8 hours before cooking.

Purée the soup using a hand-held mixer.

with salt and pepper.
8. Finely dice the ham. Add the ham to the puréed soup, and simmer for 5-10 minutes. Meanwhile, dice the bread. Melt the remaining butter, and fry the bread cubes until crisp to make croûtons.
9. Stir the cream and the reserved lentils into the soup, and bring it back to the boil. Serve in soup plates or bowls, garnished with the croûtons and with the chopped parsley, if liked.
Accompaniment: coarse rye bread.
Recommended wine: Burgundy.

EGG SOUP WITH SPINACH

SERVES 4 ■ ■

Preparation time: 45 minutes
Kcal per portion: 175
P = 11g, F = 14g, C = 2g

1 onion
2 tbsps butter
4 cups spinach
1 quart meat broth
salt
freshly ground black pepper
1 garlic clove
2 fresh sage leaves
2 tbsps heavy cream
2 tbsps freshly grated Parmesan cheese
3 cups water
2 tbsps white wine vinegar
4 eggs

1. Peel and finely chop the onion. Melt the butter, and gently fry the onion for 5 minutes until transparent.
2. Wash the spinach, and place it in a pan with the meat broth. Cover and cook over a low heat for 10 minutes, stirring occasionally.
3. Season the spinach soup with a little pepper. Peel and crush the garlic. Add the garlic, sage, cream, and cheese to the spinach.
4. Bring the water and vinegar to the boil in a pan. Break the eggs, one after another, into a soup ladle or cup, and gently slide each into the boiling water. Poach over a low heat for 3-4 minutes.
5. Remove the eggs from the liquid with a slotted spoon, drain well, and lay them on a kitchen towel. Cut around the egg white with a sharp knife to make a neat circle.
6. Pour the spinach soup into 4 soup bowls and place a poached egg in the center of each.
Accompaniment: fresh bread.
Recommended wine: Chianti classico.

BÉARNAISE SAUCE

SERVES 4 ■ ■ ■
Preparation time: 30 minutes
Kcal per portion: 375
P = 3g, F = 40g, C = 1g

3 tbsps tarragon or white
   wine vinegar
1 shallot, chopped
1-3 tsps finely chopped fresh
   tarragon
pinch of dried chervil
5 black peppercorns, crushed
⅔ cup chilled butter
3 egg yolks
salt
freshly ground black pepper
1-2 tsps lemon juice

1. Place the vinegar, shallot, 1 tsp tarragon, the chervil, and the peppercorns in a small pan. Bring to the boil, and cook until the liquid has reduced by half. Remove the pan from the heat, and set aside to cool. Strain.
2. Dice the chilled butter.
3. Place the egg yolks in a heatproof bowl or in the top of a bain-marie. Add a pinch of salt and a small piece of butter, and beat the ingredients together. Add the concentrated vinegar.
4. Set the bowl over a pan of hot water or over a bain-marie over a medium heat.
5. Beat the mixture with a whisk until thick and creamy. Do not allow the water in the bain-marie to become too hot or the sauce will separate. If necessary, remove the pan from the heat from time to time.
6. When the mixture is creamy, remove the bowl from the heat, and beat in the remaining butter, one piece at a time. Occasionally return the bowl to the pan of hot water or the bain marie to ensure that the sauce does not cool and to ensure that the butter melts.
7. When all the butter has been incorporated, season to taste with salt and pepper,

Boil the vinegar, shallots, tarragon, chervil, and peppercorns until the liquid has reduced.

Leave the spicy vinegar concentrate to cool, then strain it.

Place a heatproof bowl over a pan of hot water, and beat the egg yolks with salt and butter.

and add lemon juice to taste. Add the remaining tarragon, if liked. Serve the béarnaise sauce tepid with asparagus, fish, or meat.

LIGHT MAYONNAISE

SERVES 4 ■ ■
Preparation time: 15 minutes
Kcal per portion: 345
P = 7g, F = 35g, C = 2g

2 egg yolks
½ tsp French mustard
salt
freshly ground white pepper
½ cup peanut or sunflower oil
juice of 1 small lemon or 1-2
   tsps white wine vinegar
⅔ cup low-fat cottage cheese

1. To ensure that all the ingredients are at the same temperature, take them out of the refrigerator about 1 hour beforehand.
2. Beat together the egg yolks, mustard, and salt and pepper to taste with a whisk. Add half the oil, drop by drop, until a very thick sauce forms. (Incidentally, the bowl will not slide about on the table if you place a damp cloth underneath it.)
3. As soon as the sauce is thick and firm, stir in the lemon juice or vinegar.

> ### TIP
> *Mayonnaise may also be made in a blender, in which case 1-2 egg whites should also be added to make the sauce even lighter.*

4. Add the remaining oil in a thin stream, beating constantly, until the mayonnaise has reached the required consistency.
5. Mix with the cottage cheese, and season with salt and pepper again, if required.

CLASSIC VINAIGRETTE

SERVES 4 ■
Preparation time: 5 minutes
Kcal per portion: 180
P = trace, F = 20g, C = 0g

2 tbsps herb vinegar
salt
freshly ground black pepper
8 tbsps sunflower oil
1 tbsp finely chopped mixed
   herbs (chives, parsley,
   rosemary, thyme)

1. Season the herb vinegar with salt.
2. Beat the oil into the vinegar with a whisk. Beat the vinaigrette for 5 minutes to combine the oil and vinegar thoroughly.
3. Add the herbs, and season the vinaigrette to taste with pepper.
4. This vinaigrette goes best of all with tender green salads, but it is also delicious

Combine the salt and herb vinegar, then add the oil and mix well with a whisk.

with fish or meat salad. It may be used as a dressing for appetizers.

WHITE BUTTER SAUCE
Beurre blanc

SERVES 6 ■ ■ ■
Preparation time: 15 minutes
Kcal per portion: 245
P = 0.5g, F = 25g, C = 2g

4 shallots, chopped
1 tsp coarsely ground black
   pepper
2 tbsps mirepoix – finely
   chopped vegetables sautéed
   in butter (optional)
½ cup white wine vinegar
½ cup white wine or fish
   consommé
⅔ cup chilled butter
2 tbsps heavy cream
salt
freshly ground white pepper

1. Place the shallots, black pepper, mirepoix, if using, vinegar, and wine or consommé in a small pan and bring to the boil. Cook until the liquid has reduced by half.
2. Strain the reduced liquid into a saucepan, and boil until it has reduced by a further two-thirds.
3. Dice the chilled butter.
4. Bring the reduced liquid back to the boil, and add the cream. Gradually beat in the butter, 1 piece at a time, until the sauce is creamy. Do not allow the sauce to boil. Season to taste with salt and pepper.
5. This sauce goes well with fish, such as sea-bream, trout, and turbot.

> ### TIP
> *The sauce should be served on heated plates, otherwise it will separate very quickly.*

Add the shallots and pepper to the vinegar and white wine, and boil to reduce the liquid.

Dice the well-chilled butter.

After bringing the reduced liquid to the boil, add the cream.

Gradually stir in the pieces of butter, using a whisk.

LIGHT MOREL CREAM SAUCE

SERVES 4 ■ ■ ■
Preparation time: 55 minutes
Soaking time: 2 hours
Kcal per portion: 285
P = 3g, F = 22g, C = 10g

2 tbsps dried morel
   mushrooms
1 tbsp butter
1 tbsp finely chopped shallots
½ cup sherry or port
1 cup heavy cream
salt
freshly ground black pepper
pinch of cayenne pepper

1. Place the morels in a bowl, cover with cold water, and set aside to soak for 2 hours. Drain and reserve the soaking water. Pour it through a coffee filter paper to remove all particles of dirt, and set aside.
2. If necessary, cut the morels in halves or in quarters. Place the morels and the strained soaking liquid in a pan and bring to the boil. Cook for about 20 minutes until tender.
3. Melt the butter, and gently fry the shallots until transparent.
4. Add the sherry or port and the morel cooking water. Rub the mixture through a sieve and return to the pan. Bring to the boil, and cook vigorously to reduce. Add the morels and cream.
5. Continue boiling the sauce until it becomes creamy. Season to taste with salt, pepper, and the cayenne pepper.
6. Serve the morel sauce with pasta and vegetable or meat dishes.

MILD MUSTARD SAUCE

SERVES 4 ■
Preparation time: 20 minutes
Kcal per portion: 20
P = 1g, F = 1g, C = 1g

1 cup meat broth
2 tsps Dijon mustard
1 tbsp coarse-grain mustard
⅔ cup sour cream
1 tsp chopped fresh tarragon
3 tbsps heavy cream
pinch of sugar
salt
freshly ground black pepper

1. Boil the meat broth to reduce the liquid by half.
2. Beat together both mustards, the sour cream, and tarragon. Set aside to stand for 15 minutes.
3. Add the cream to the meat broth, and boil for 2-3 minutes to reduce the liquid. Stir in the mustard and sour cream mixture, and heat gently without allowing it to boil. Remove the pan from the heat, stir in the sugar, and season to taste with salt and pepper.

> ### TIP
> *The flavorings dissolve in the cold sour cream. That is why the mustard should not be boiled, as this will make it sharp. Treated carefully, it will stay aromatic.*

4. Serve this mustard sauce with meat, fish, or boiled eggs. If serving with fish, reduce the quantity of mustard by half and omit the tarragon. Before serving, sprinkle chives over the sauce.

**MILD
MUSTARD SAUCE**

CURRY SAUCE WITH CHUTNEY

SERVES 4 ■■
Preparation time: 1 hour
Kcal per portion: 80
P = 1g, F = 4g, C = 8g

2 tbsps butter
1 large onion, finely chopped
2-3 tbsps mild curry powder
¾ cup meat broth
1 apple
¾ cup milk
1 tsp cornstarch
6 tbsps pineapple juice
1 tbsp mango chutney
2-3 lemon balm leaves
1 tbsp brandy (optional)
salt
freshly ground black pepper

1. Melt the butter, and gently fry the onion until transparent.
2. Stir in the curry powder and add ⅔ cup of the broth.
3. Peel and finely grate the apple. Stir the apple into the sauce.
4. Add the milk, bring to the boil, lower the heat, and simmer for about 30 minutes.
5. Mix together the cornstarch and the remaining broth. Stir it into the sauce, and cook, stirring constantly, until thick and creamy.
6. Stir in the pineapple juice, mango chutney, and lemon balm, and season to taste with salt and pepper. Stir in the brandy, if using. This sauce goes with meat and chicken dishes or hard-boiled eggs.

> **TIP**
>
> *A curry sauce may be varied by adding shredded coconut, apple, or banana – and even milk or yogurt.*

CHAMPAGNE SAUCE

SERVES 4 ■■
Preparation time: 25 minutes
Kcal per portion: 305
P = 2g, F = 27g, C = 4g

1 cup chicken or fish broth
1 shallot, finely chopped
12 peppercorns, crushed
1 cup champagne or
*   sparkling white wine*
1 cup heavy cream
2 tbsps chilled butter

Add some of the champagne or wine, the chopped shallot, salt, and pepper to the reduced broth.

1. Boil the chicken or fish broth until the liquid has reduced by half.
2. Add the shallot, peppercorns and ¾ cup of the champagne or wine. Boil until only 6 tbsps of liquid remain. Strain the reduced liquid into a clean pan.
3. Add the cream, and boil until the sauce becomes thick and creamy. Stir in the remaining champagne or wine.
4. Dice the chilled butter. Beat the butter into the sauce, 1 piece at a time, with a whisk. Season to taste with salt and pepper.
5. Champagne sauce tastes best of all served with fish.

ORANGE SAUCE

SERVES 4 ■■
Preparation time: 30 minutes
Kcal per portion: 105
P = 1g, F = 4g, C = 9g

grated rind of 1 orange
1 cup orange juice
2 tbsps soy sauce
6 tbsps concentrated veal
*   broth*
6 tbsps dry sherry
1 tbsp cornstarch
2 tsps orange marmalade
salt
freshly ground black pepper
pinch of cayenne pepper
1 tbsp chilled butter

1. Place the orange rind and orange juice in a small pan, and boil until the liquid has reduced by half.
2. Add the soy sauce and broth, and boil for a further 2-3 minutes. Mix together the sherry and cornstarch. Stir the cornstarch mixture into the sauce and boil, stirring constantly, until the sauce is clear and slightly thickened.
3. Stir in the marmalade, and season to taste with salt and pepper (remember, the soy sauce is very salty), and add the cayenne pepper.
4. Dice the butter, and gently stir it into the sauce, 1 piece at a time.
5. This sauce goes well with chicken, lamb, and fillet of pork or veal; in this case, the juice from cooking the meat may be used instead of broth. Mix the meat juice with half the sherry.

RED WINE SAUCE WITH SHALLOTS

SERVES 4 ■■
Preparation time: 35 minutes
Kcal per portion: 160
P = 8g, F = 11g, C = 1g

3 shallots or 1 onion
4 tbsps butter
⅔ cup meat broth
4 beef marrow bones
1 cup red wine
3 tbsps concentrated veal
*   broth or clear gravy*
salt
freshly ground black pepper
1 tbsp chopped fresh parsley
*   (optional)*

1. Peel and finely chop the shallots or onion. Melt 2 tbsps of the butter, and gently fry the shallots or onion for 5 minutes.
2. Place the broth in a pan and bring to the boil. Add the marrow bones, and simmer briefly – the marrow should remain pink. Leave it in the broth to keep warm.

> **TIP**
>
> *This sauce also goes well with strongly flavored fish.*

3. Boil the shallots or the onion in ¾ cup of the red wine until the liquid has reduced to 6 tbsps.
4. Add the remaining wine and the veal broth or clear gravy and bring to the boil. Boil the mixture until it has reduced by half.
5. Rub the sauce through a sieve. Dice the remaining butter, and stir it into the sauce, 1 piece at a time.
6. Season to taste with salt and pepper, and stir in the marrow.
7. Serve this sauce with fried fish. It may be garnished with parsley.

Wholefood Recipes

*I*n this chapter, Doris-Katharina Hessler shows how soups, stews, delicate whips and, particularly, sauces play a central role in her wholefood cuisine repertoire. With delicious new ideas for dishes like Tomato and Chickpea Stew with Lamb, and Lentil Stew with Ginger and Smoked Eel, you are guaranteed to be tempted by this selection. Wholefood cuisine has a truly spectacular contribution to make on the subject of sauces too, offering, for instance, Buttermilk Sauce with Avocado and Capers, or Pommery Mustard Sauce.

Tomato and Chickpea Stew with Lamb
(recipe page 80)

CURRIED MUSSEL SOUP WITH LYCHEES

SERVES 4 ■■

*Preparation time: 1 hour
10 minutes
Kcal per serving: 690
P = 13g, F = 39g, C = 25g*

9 cups mussels in their shells
2 leeks
4 sticks celery
2 carrots
3 tbsps sunflower oil
1 quart water
1 quart dry white wine
salt
freshly ground white pepper
1 cup sour cream
3 tbsps sherry vinegar
3 tbsps dry French vermouth
2 bananas
2 tsps curry powder
40 lychees
1 cup light cream

Boil the mussels with the leeks, celery, and carrots until the shells open.

Remove the mussels from the shells and set aside.

Add the leek strips and banana, then the lychees and the mussels to the soup.

1. Scrub the mussels under cold running water and cut away the beards. Discard any that do not close immediately when sharply tapped. Drain.

2. Set 1 leek aside. Trim, wash, and chop the remaining leeks. Trim, wash, and chop the celery. Peel and chop the carrots. Heat the oil, and gently fry the leek, celery, and carrots. Add the water and wine, season to taste with salt and pepper, and bring to the boil over a high heat.

3. Add the mussels, and cook until the shells open. Remove them from the pan with a slotted spoon, and discard any that have not opened. Continue boiling the cooking liquid over a high heat until it has reduced by half. Remove the mussels from their shells.

4. Rub the reduced cooking liquid through a sieve. Return to the pan and stir in the sour cream, vinegar, and vermouth. Simmer over a medium heat for 5 minutes.

5. Trim and wash the remaining leek and cut into matchstick strips. Peel and thinly slice the banana.

6. Add the leek, banana, and curry powder to the soup, and simmer over a low heat for 5 minutes.

7. Peel the lychees. Add the lychees and the mussels to the soup and heat through gently. Whip the cream, and gently fold it into the soup. Serve immediately.

CREAM OF MUSHROOM SOUP

SERVES 4 ■■

*Preparation time: 45 minutes
Kcal per serving: 540
P = 7g, F = 52g, C = 11g*

1 bunch green onions
 (scallions)
6 cups wild mushrooms (e.g.
 chanterelles or porcini)
5 tbsps sunflower oil
6 cups beef, chicken, or
 vegetable broth
2 cups heavy cream
salt
freshly ground white pepper
1 shallot
3 tbsps snipped fresh chives

Gently fry the green onions, together with most of the mushrooms in 3 tbsps of oil.

Add the broth and cream, and season with salt and pepper.

Rub the puréed soup through a fine sieve using a tablespoon.

Sauté the remaining mushrooms and the chopped shallot in the remaining oil.

1. Trim, wash, and slice the green onions. Wipe and finely chop the mushrooms.

2. Heat 3 tbsps of the oil in a pan, add the onions and 4 cups of the mushrooms, and gently fry for a few minutes. Add the broth and 1 cup of the cream, and season to taste with salt and pepper. Simmer over a medium heat for about 15 minutes.

3. Purée the soup in a blender, rub it through a sieve, and return it to the pan. Heat it through again. Taste and adjust the seasoning.

4. Peel and finely chop the shallot. Heat the remaining oil in a skillet, and gently fry the shallot and the remaining mushrooms for 3-5 minutes. Season to taste with salt and pepper.

5. Whip the remaining cream, add it to the soup, and beat the soup with a hand-held mixer until it is frothy.

6. Divide the mushroom and shallot mixture between 4 soup plates or bowls, pour over the mushroom soup and garnish with chives. Serve immediately.

TOMATO AND CHICK-PEA STEW WITH LAMB

(photograph page 76/77)

SERVES 4 ■■
Preparation time: 1 hour
Soaking time: overnight
Kcal per serving: 755
P = 48g, F = 47g, C = 34g

1 cup chickpeas (garbanzo
    beans)
3½ pounds leg of lamb, boned
    (ask your butcher for the
    bone for making broth)
1 bunch green onions
    (scallions)
2 garlic cloves
1 red chili
6 ripe beefsteak tomatoes
4 tbsps olive oil
2 cups canned tomatoes,
    chopped and drained
salt
1½ quarts strong beef broth
2 tbsps torn basil leaves

Place the chickpeas in plenty of salted water and boil for about 10 minutes.

Fry the lamb on all sides in hot olive oil over a high heat.

1. Place the chickpeas in a bowl, cover with cold water, and set aside overnight to soak. Trim the lamb and cut into bite-sized pieces.
2. Trim, wash, and finely dice the green onions. Peel and finely dice the garlic. Halve, seed, and finely dice the chili. Wash and quarter the beefsteak tomatoes.
3. Heat the oil in a large pan, add the lamb, and fry it on all sides for a few minutes over a high heat. Remove the lamb, cover, and set aside. Add the lamb bone, onions, garlic, and chili to the pan, and fry for 5 minutes. Add the tomatoes. Mix together thoroughly, and add the broth. Simmer over a medium heat for 15 minutes.
4. Boil the chickpeas in salted water for about 10 minutes. Drain.
5. Rub the broth through a sieve, and return it to the pan. Add the lamb, and simmer over a medium heat for about 20 minutes. Stir in the chickpeas, and bring briefly to the boil. Stir in the basil and serve.
Recommended drink: lager or rosé wine.

EXOTIC RICE STEW

SERVES 4 ■
Preparation time: 1 hour
Kcal per serving: 370
P = 9g, F = 10g, C = 57g

2 carrots
1 kohlrabi
4 leeks
1 head Chinese (Nappa)
    cabbage
3 tbsps sesame oil
1 red chili, seeded and finely
    chopped
2 tbsps finely chopped root
    ginger
2 quarts strong chicken broth
½ cup sake (rice wine) or dry
    sherry
4 tsps soy sauce
1 cup long-grain rice
1 tbsp chopped fresh
    coriander
salt
freshly ground white pepper

1. Peel and slice the carrots and kohlrabi. Cut the slices into matchstick strips. Trim and wash the leeks and Chinese cabbage. Cut the leeks and Chinese cabbage into matchstick strips.
2. Heat the oil in a pan, and gently fry the carrot, kohlrabi, leek, Chinese cabbage, chili and ginger for 5 minutes. Add the broth, sake or sherry and soy sauce. Stir in the rice and coriander, and season to taste with salt and pepper. Cover and simmer over a low heat for 15-20 minutes until the rice is cooked. Serve immediately.
Recommended wine: Muscatel.

LENTIL STEW WITH GINGER & SMOKED EEL

SERVES 4 ■■
Preparation time: 1 hour
Soaking time: 1-2 hours
Kcal per serving: 605
P = 34g, F = 37g, C = 30g

1 cup green or yellow lentils
2 sticks celery
1 red onion
2 tbsps sunflower oil
3 tbsps sherry vinegar
1 quart strong beef or veal
    broth
½ cup dry white wine
salt
freshly ground white pepper
3 tbsps root ginger, peeled
    and finely chopped
½ tsp curry powder
1¾ pounds smoked eel
4 parsley sprigs

1. Place the lentils in a bowl, cover with cold water and set aside to soak for 1-2 hours. Transfer the lentils and their soaking water to a pan, bring to the boil, lower the heat, and simmer for 30-40 minutes until just tender. Alternatively, cook them in their soaking water for 10 minutes in a pressure cooker. Drain.
2. Trim, wash, and finely chop the celery. Peel and finely dice the onion.
3. Heat the oil in a pan, and gently fry the celery, onion, and lentils for a few minutes. Add the vinegar, broth, and wine, season to taste with salt and pepper, and stir in the ginger and curry powder. Cover and simmer over a medium heat until the celery is tender but still firm to the bite.
4. Skin the smoked eel and remove the flesh from the central bone. Chop the flesh into pieces.
5. Serve the lentil stew in deep plates and divide the smoked eel between them. Garnish with parsley.
Recommended wine: a full-bodied white wine.

SWEET-AND-SOUR GINGER DIP

SERVES 4 ■
Preparation time: 5 minutes
Kcal per serving: 100
P = 1g, F = 5g, C = 12g

½ cup sour cream
5 tbsps apricot jam
grated rind and juice of 1
   lemon
2 tsps freshly grated root
   ginger
¼ tsp vanilla extract
4 tsps white port
1 tsp sugar or fructose
salt
freshly ground white pepper
2 tbsps heavy cream

Thoroughly combine the sour cream, jam, lemon rind, lemon juice, ginger, vanilla extract, port, and sugar or fructose, and season to taste with salt and pepper. Whip the cream until stiff, and fold into the mixture. Serve as an accompaniment to raw vegetables, fondue, or shellfish.

POMMERY MUSTARD DIP

SERVES 4 ■
Preparation time: 5 minutes
Kcal per serving: 140
P = 1g, F = 13g, C = 2g

½ cup crème fraîche
½ tsp English mustard
   powder
2 tbsps pommery mustard
4 tsps dry French vermouth
ground sea salt
juice of ½ lemon

Combine the ingredients, mixing them together thoroughly. Serve with raw vegetables or fondue.

TOMATO SAUCE

SERVES 4 ■ ■
Preparation time: 30 minutes
Kcal per serving: 140
P = 2g, F = 10g, C = 7g

3 beefsteak tomatoes
1 onion
1 bunch tarragon
4 tbsps olive oil
2 cups canned tomatoes,
   chopped
2 tsps tarragon vinegar
4 tsps dry French vermouth
salt
freshly ground white pepper
pinch of sugar

1. Blanch, skin, and seed the tomatoes. Remove the stalk bases and reserve all the trimmings. Finely dice the flesh.
2. Peel and chop the onion. Pick the tarragon leaves from the stems. Finely chop one-third of the leaves, and set aside. Roughly chop the remaining leaves and the stems.
3. Heat the olive oil in a skillet, and lightly fry the onion for 5 minutes. Add the tomato trimmings, canned tomatoes and their juice, the roughly chopped tarragon, vinegar, and vermouth. Season to taste with salt and pepper, and stir in the sugar. Simmer the mixture for 5 minutes.
4. Rub the sauce through a sieve. Add the diced tomato and finely chopped tarragon leaves. Adjust the seasoning, if necessary. This sauce goes well with pasta dishes or as a spicy dip for raw vegetables.

TIP

*The tarragon
may be replaced
by fresh basil.*

Tarragon is a strong-tasting herb which gives soups and sauces an exquisite aroma.

Dice the skinned beefsteak tomatoes, removing the seeds and stalk bases.

Peel and chop the onion, then lightly fry in oil.

Add the tomato trimmings, canned tomatoes, vinegar, vermouth, and seasoning to the onion, and cook for 5 minutes.

BUTTERMILK SAUCE WITH AVOCADOS AND CAPERS

SERVES 4 ■
Preparation time: 20 minutes
Kcal per serving: 340
P = 4g, F = 34g, C = 4g

1 garlic clove
2 ripe avocados
½ cup heavy cream
½ cup buttermilk
juice of 1 lemon
1 shallot
2 anchovy fillets
3 tbsps capers
4 tbsps snipped chives
salt
freshly ground white pepper
1 tsp Dijon mustard

1. Peel the garlic. Peel and pit the avocados, and finely dice 1 of them. Purée the remaining avocado flesh with the cream, buttermilk, lemon juice, and garlic. Rub the mixture through a sieve.
2. Peel and finely chop the shallot. Finely dice the anchovy fillets. Stir the shallot, anchovies, capers, and chives into the sauce. Season to taste with salt and pepper, and stir in the mustard. Stir in the diced avocado. Serve the sauce with egg dishes, cold roasts, or fish dishes.

TIP

*Prepare this
sauce shortly
before serving, as
it discolors
quickly. The
avocados used
should be fully
ripe.*

DRESSING FOR GREEN SALADS AND VEGETABLE SALADS

SERVES 4 ■
Preaparation time: 5 minutes
Kcal per serving: 75
P = 5g, F = 5g, C = 2g

½ cup yogurt, crème fraîche,
   buttermilk, kefir, or sour
   cream
2 tsps French mustard
2 tbsps sunflower oil
2 tbsps white wine or herb
   vinegar
1 shallot, peeled and
   chopped
salt
freshly ground white pepper
2 tbsps mustard sprouts

Combine all the ingredients
thoroughly.

DRESSING FOR FISH OR EGG DISHES

SERVES 4 ■
Preparation time: 5 minutes
Kcal per serving: 105
P = 0g, F = 10g, C = 0g

½ cup yogurt, crème fraîche,
   buttermilk, kefir or sour
   cream
4 tsps dry French vermouth
1 tsp French mustard
4 tbsps sunflower oil
2 tbsps white wine vinegar
1 cup chopped mixed herbs,
   such as basil, dill, chervil,
   and parsley
1 shallot, peeled and
   chopped
salt
freshly ground white pepper

Combine all the ingredients
thoroughly.

*Endive (Belgian Endive or Witloof)
has a slightly bitter taste, which is
made milder by the addition of a
dressing.*

Avocados contain valuable fats.

DRESSING FOR POTATO OR AVOCADO SALADS

SERVES 4 ■
Preparation time: 10 minutes
Kcal per serving: 125
P = 5g, F = 10g, C = 3g

½ cup yogurt, crème fraîche,
   buttermilk, kefir, or sour
   cream
1 tsp tomato paste
4 tbsps olive oil
2 tbsps white wine vinegar
1 shallot, peeled and
   chopped
salt
freshly ground white pepper
4 tbsps cress
2 tomatoes, peeled and diced

Thoroughly combine the
yogurt, crème fraîche, buttermilk, kefir or soured
cream, tomato paste, oil,
vinegar, and shallot, and season to taste with salt and
pepper. Stir in the cress and
diced tomato.

SALAD DRESSINGS MADE WITH EGG

SERVES 4 ■
*Preparation time: depending
on method, 5-10 minutes*
Kcal per serving: 320
P = 3g, F = 34g, C = 0g

4 egg yolks
1 tsp herb mustard
4 tsps white wine vinegar
3 tbsps white wine
1 cup sunflower oil
salt
freshly ground white pepper

Method 1: Make sure all the
ingredients are at the same
temperature. Place them all
in a high-sided mixing bowl,
and beat with a hand-held
mixer to make a smooth
mayonnaise.
Method 2: Make sure the
egg yolk, mustard, vinegar,
and wine are all at the same
temperature. Place them in a
mixing bowl and beat with
an egg whisk until the mixture is creamy. Gradually
beat in the oil, adding it drop
by drop, until a creamy mayonnaise forms. Season with
salt and pepper.

VARIATIONS
CURRY MAYONNAISE

Kcal per serving: 320
P = 3g, F = 33g, C = 0g

4 egg yolks
2 tbsps curry powder
4 tsps white wine vinegar
3 tbsps white wine
1 cup sunflower oil
salt
freshly ground white pepper

Prepare following method 1
or 2 in the basic recipe. Use
for dressing vegetable salads
or serve with poultry dishes.

OLIVE MAYONNAISE

Kcal per serving: 330
P = 3g, F = 35g, C = 0g

4 egg yolks
2 tsps chopped black olives
2 tbsps balsamic vinegar
1 cup olive oil
salt
2 tbsps sour cream

Prepare following method 1
or 2 in the basic recipe, finally folding in the sour cream.
Serve with pasta dishes and
broiled meats.

PEPPER MAYONNAISE

Kcal per serving: 360
P = 3g, F = 38g, C = 0g

4 egg yolks
4 tsps brandy
4 tsps cider vinegar
1 cup sunflower oil
salt
freshly ground white pepper
2 tbsps each, pickled green
   and pink peppercorns
2 tbsps sour cream

Prepare following method 1
or 2 in the basic recipe, finally stirring in the peppercorns
and cream. This mayonnaise
goes well with egg and
cheese dishes.

GARLIC MAYONNAISE

Kcal per serving: 310
P = 3g, F = 33g, C = 0g

4 egg yolks
4 tsps white wine vinegar
3 tbsps white wine
1 cup olive oil
2 garlic cloves, crushed
1 tsp each, chopped fresh
   rosemary, thyme, and sage
salt
freshly ground white pepper

Prepare following method 1
or 2 in the basic recipe.

ASIAN DRESSING

SERVES 4 ■

Preparation time: 20 minutes
Kcal per serving: 140
P = 1g, F = 13g, C = 3g

1 onion
1 garlic clove
¼ red pepper
¼ green pepper
¼ yellow pepper
4 tbsps canned unsweetened
*   or fresh coconut milk*
2 tbsps soy sauce
1 tsp freshly grated root
*   ginger*
1 tsp chopped fresh coriander
*   (cilanto)*
salt
freshly ground black pepper
2 tbsps sherry vinegar
4 tbsps sesame oil

1. Peel and finely chop the onion and garlic. Finely dice the red, green, and yellow peppers.

Onion and peppers are the main ingredients for this dressing.

2. Place the remaining ingredients in a bowl and mix thoroughly with a whisk. Add the onion, garlic, and peppers, and set aside to marinate for a short while. Serve with raw fish, preferably on a base of lettuce leaves, or with cold roast chicken, or as a dip with raw mixed vegetables.

AVOCADO OLIVE CREAM

SERVES 4 ■

Preparation time: 20 minutes
Kcal per serving: 500
P = 3g, F = 53g, C = 2g

2 egg yolks
½ cup olive oil
juice of 1 lemon
2 garlic cloves
⅔ cup pitted black olives
1 avocado
3 tbsps finely chopped fresh
*   basil*
salt
freshly ground white pepper

1. Place the egg yolks in a bowl and beat in the oil and lemon juice with a whisk.
2. Peel and finely chop the garlic. Finely chop the olives. Peel, halve, and pit the avocado. Purée the flesh. Stir the garlic, olives, avocado and basil into the frothy egg sauce, and season to taste with salt and pepper.

VARIATIONS
EGG DIP

1 egg yolk
½ tsp Dijon mustard
4 tbsps red wine vinegar
5 tbsps olive oil
2 tbsps diced tomato
2 tbsps capers
1 tbsp chopped fresh parsley

Prepare in the same way as the Avocado Olive Cream. Both sauces make ideal dips for raw vegetables and fondues.

Fresh basil leaves give salad dressings a delicious aroma.

Beat the egg yolk vigorously, slowly pouring in the olive oil at the same time.

Ripe avocado is easy to separate from the stone.

To make the egg dip, combine the egg yolk, mustard, vinegar, and olive oil using a hand-held mixer.

MANGO AND CORIANDER VINAIGRETTE

SERVES 4 ■

Preparation time: 20 minutes
Kcal per serving: 125
P = 0g, F = 10g, C = 8g

1 ripe mango
1 yellow chili
salt
freshly ground white pepper
2 tbsps white wine vinegar
4 tbsps sunflower oil
2 tbsps chopped fresh
*   coriander (cilanto)*

1. Peel the mango, cut the flesh away from the stone, and finely dice. Halve, seed, and finely chop the chili.
2. Beat together the salt and vinegar, then gradually beat in the oil. Stir in the mango, chili and coriander, and season to taste with pepper.

The flesh of the mango is hard to separate from the stone; the best method is to cut it away from the center in thin slices.

This sauce is delicious served with cold chicken or roast veal.

Quick-and-easy Recipes

This chapter is for those who have only a short lunch break, for those who have no wish to stand slaving over a hot stove at the end of a day's work, and for anyone needing to entertain surprise guests. It is full of ideas for quick soups, stews, and sauces – whose flavor will not betray how easy they are to prepare. There is no need to skimp on fresh vegetables and herbs; Tomato and Garlic Soup or Cream of Basil Soup with Cherry Tomatoes can be ready in 20 minutes, while Fish Stew with Vegetables and Saffron takes no longer than half an hour to prepare. Moreover, recipes such as Cream of Trout Soup or Cream of Horseradish Soup with Strips of Salmon prove that when cooking in a hurry, there is no need to cut down on sophistication.

Chilled Garlic and Herb Sauce
(recipe page 98)

TRANSPARENT NOODLE SOUP WITH BREAST OF CHICKEN

SERVES 4 ■
Preparation time: 25 minutes
Kcal per serving: 230
P = 33g, F = 3g, C = 18g

4 ounces transparent noodles
1 quart chicken broth
1 bunch lemon balm
4 chicken breast fillets
salt
freshly ground white pepper
1 cup button mushrooms
1 garlic clove
juice of ½ lemon

1. Pour boiling water over the transparent noodles and set aside for 10 minutes.
2. Slowly bring the chicken broth to the boil.
3. Wash the lemon balm, and shake dry. Set aside 2 sprigs for the garnish. Add the remainder to the chicken broth, and simmer for 10 minutes.
4. Skin the chicken breast fillets and cut crosswise into strips. Season to taste with salt and pepper. Wipe and thinly slice the mushrooms.
5. Drain the transparent noodles and, while still in the sieve, snip them with a pair of scissors.

T I P

Shrimp may be used instead of chicken breast. In this case, replace the lemon balm with chervil.

6. Remove and discard the lemon balm from the chicken broth. Add the transparent noodles, strips of chicken breast, and the mushrooms, and simmer for 10 minutes.

Lemon balm gives the soup a fresh, fruity flavor.

Place the transparent noodles in a pan and pour over boiling water.

After 10 minutes, drain off the water and snip the transparent noodles.

7. Peel the garlic and crush it into the soup. Add the lemon juice, and season to taste with salt and pepper. Pick the remaining lemon balm leaves from the stems. Pour the soup into 4 bowls, scatter over the lemon balm and serve.

CREAM OF BROCCOLI SOUP WITH PINENUTS

SERVES 4 ■
Preparation time: 25 minutes
Kcal per serving: 225
P = 8g, F = 19g, C = 7g

1½ pounds frozen broccoli, thawed
1 onion
2 tbsps butter
2 garlic cloves
3 cups meat broth
1 cup heavy cream
salt
freshly ground black pepper
1 tsp fresh or ½ tsp dried oregano
3 tbsps pinenuts

1. Wash and roughly chop the broccoli, reserving a few attractive flowerets. Peel and finely chop the onion.
2. Melt half of the butter in a skillet, and gently fry the broccoli and onion for 5 minutes.
3. Peel the garlic and crush it into the pan. Add the broth and the cream, bring to the boil, cover, and simmer over a low heat for 15 minutes.
4. Purée the soup in a blender or with a hand-held mixer. Season to taste with salt and pepper and stir in the oregano.
5. Melt the remaining butter, and fry the pinenuts until golden-brown.
6. Add the remaining broccoli flowerets to the soup. Serve in bowls or deep plates and sprinkle over the pinenuts. Cauliflower or calabrese may be used instead of broccoli, and the pinenuts may be replaced by sesame seeds.

FENNEL SOUP WITH STRIPS OF HAM

SERVES 4 ■
Preparation time: 30 minutes
Kcal per serving: 225
P = 16g, F = 14g, C = 9g

4 fennel bulbs
2 tbsps butter
1 tsp fennel seeds
1 quart vegetable broth
salt
freshly ground white pepper
juice of ½ lemon
8 ounces cooked ham, thickly sliced

1. Trim and wash the fennel, and set the leaves aside. Cut the bulb in half lengthwise, then chop it into matchstick strips.
2. Melt the butter in a pan, and gently fry the fennel seeds for 1-2 minutes. Add the fennel, and fry for a fur-

Chop the fennel leaves off the bulb and set aside; they make an ideal garnish.

ther 3-4 minutes. Add the vegetable broth and bring to the boil. Lower the heat and simmer for 15 minutes. Season to taste with salt and pepper and stir in the lemon juice.
3. Trim the ham, cut in half lengthwise and then into matchstick strips. Add the ham to the soup.
4. Finely chop the fennel leaves. Serve the soup sprinkled with the fennel leaves.

FRENCH BREAD SOUP

SERVES 4

Preparation time: 30 minutes
Kcal per serving: 160
P = 4g, F = 6g, C = 18g

2 onions
2 tbsps lard or shortening
2 day-old French sticks
½ cup lite beer
3 cups meat broth
salt
freshly ground black pepper
freshly grated nutmeg
3 tbsps snipped fresh chives

1. Peel the onions, and finely chop 1 onion. Melt half the lard or shortening in a skillet, and fry the chopped onion for 5-7 minutes.
2. Cut the French bread into slices about ¼ inch thick. Add them to the pan, and fry for a further 5 minutes.
3. Add the beer and broth, cover and simmer for 15 minutes.
4. Meanwhile, thinly slice the remaining onion and push out into rings. Melt the remaining lard or shortening, and stir-fry the rings until brown.

> ### TIP
> *If French bread is not available, use kaiser rolls.*

5. Season the soup to taste with salt, pepper, and nutmeg. Add the onion rings, cover and simmer for a further 5 minutes.
6. Serve the soup in individual bowls, garnished with the chives.

Gently fry the chopped onion before adding the sliced French bread.

Pour the beer and the meat broth over the French bread.

A mandolin, vegetable slicer, or food processor produces very thin onion rings.

Stir-fry the onion rings in lard or shortening until they turn brown.

CREAM OF ASPARAGUS SOUP WITH CRESS

SERVES 4

Preparation time: 30 minutes
Kcal per serving: 200
P = 4g, F = 20g, C = 3g

1¼ pounds asparagus
2 tbsps butter
1 carton of cress
¾ cup crème fraîche
3 cups vegetable broth
salt
freshly ground white pepper
freshly grated nutmeg
1 tbsp lemon juice

1. Trim and wash the asparagus. Cut off the tips and set aside. Peel and slice the stems.
2. Melt the butter in a saucepan, and gently fry the asparagus stems for 5 minutes.
3. Rinse and snip the cress. Reserve a little for the garnish, and stir the remainder into the pan.
4. Add the crème fraîche and vegetable broth, and simmer for 10 minutes. Season to taste with salt, pepper, and nutmeg.
5. Meanwhile, cook the asparagus tips in lightly salted boiling water for 3 minutes until tender but still firm to the bite. Refresh in ice-cold water and drain thoroughly.
6. Purée the soup with a hand-held mixer or in a food processor. Return to the pan, bring to the boil and add the lemon juice and asparagus tips. Heat through.
7. Serve in soup plates, garnished with the remaining cress.
The same recipe may be used to make a cream of kohlrabi soup, in which case croûtons may be used as a garnish.

TOMATO AND GARLIC SOUP

SERVES 4

Preparation time: 20 minutes
Kcal per serving: 300
P = 6g, F = 27g, C = 7g

6 slices smoked streaky
* bacon, rind removed*
1 tbsp vegetable oil
5-6 garlic cloves
4 cups canned tomatoes,
* sieved*
salt
freshly ground black pepper
3 tbsps snipped fresh chives

1. Cut the bacon into matchstick strips.
2. Heat the oil in a skillet, and fry the bacon strips for 5-6 minutes until cooked.
3. Meanwhile, peel and thinly slice the garlic. Add to the pan, and gently fry over a low heat until golden.
4. Add the tomatoes, slowly bring to the boil and simmer for 10 minutes. Season to taste with salt and pepper.

> ### TIP
> *If enough time is available, fresh, beefsteak tomatoes may be used. They should be skinned, seeded, chopped, gently fried, and then puréed.*

5. Pour the soup into 4 individual soup bowls, garnish with the chives, and serve immediately. If liked, substitute smoked turkey breast for the bacon.

CREAM OF TROUT SOUP

SERVES 4
Preparation time: 20 minutes
Kcal per serving: 300
P = 31g, F = 18g, C = 2g

1 onion
1 tbsp butter
6 smoked trout fillets
1 cup heavy cream
3 cups fish broth
salt
freshly ground white pepper
1 tbsp lemon juice
2 egg yolks
2 tbsp chopped fresh dill

1. Peel and finely chop the onion. Melt the butter in a

Remove pan from heat, and stir beaten egg yolk into the soup.

pan, and gently fry the onion over a low heat for 5-7 minutes until soft.
2. Divide the trout fillets into pieces. Reserve a few small pieces for the garnish, if liked, and purée the remainder with the cream in a food processor.
3. Add the trout purée and the fish broth to the pan, and slowly bring the mixture to the boil. Simmer over a low heat for 5 minutes. Season with salt and pepper, and stir in the lemon juice.
4. Beat the egg yolks. Remove the pan from the heat, and stir in the egg yolks.
5. Beat the soup briefly until frothy. Sprinkle with the dill, then pour the soup into deep plates or bowls. If liked, garnish with trout fillet.

CREAM OF HORSERADISH SOUP WITH STRIPS OF SALMON

SERVES 4
Preparation time: 20 minutes
Kcal per serving: 280
P = 16g, F = 22g, C = 4g

1 small onion
1 tbsp butter
5 tbsps creamed horseradish
1 cup full-fat cream cheese
1 quart vegetable broth
salt
freshly ground white pepper
1 tbsp lemon juice
6 ounces smoked salmon, sliced
1 carton of cress

1. Peel and finely chop the onion. Melt the butter in a skillet, and gently fry the onion for 5-7 minutes until soft.
2. Stir in the horseradish and cream cheese. Cook over a low heat, stirring constantly, until the cheese begins to melt.
3. Add the broth, bring to the boil and simmer, uncovered, for 10 minutes, beating with a whisk from time to time. Season to taste with salt and pepper, and stir in the lemon juice.
4. Cut the smoked salmon into matchstick strips.
5. Rinse and snip the cress. Reserve a little for the garnish, and stir the remainder into the soup.
6. Pour the soup into deep plates or bowls, add the strips of salmon and garnish with the remaining cress.

SPICY BEAN SOUP WITH ZUCCHINI

SERVES 4
Preparation time: 30 minutes
Kcal per serving: 440
P = 29g, F = 8g, C = 63g

1 large onion
2 tbsps olive oil
2 x 14 ounce cans red kidney beans
3 tbsps tomato paste
½ tsp chili powder
pinch of cayenne pepper
salt
freshly ground black pepper
3 cups meat broth
12 very small zucchini

1. Peel and chop the onion. Heat the olive oil, and gently fry the onion for 5-7 minutes until transparent.
2. Drain the beans, rinse with cold water, and drain again.
3. Stir the tomato paste into the pan and cook for a further 2 minutes. Add the beans, chili powder and cayenne pepper, and season to taste with salt and pepper.
4. Add the broth and slowly bring to the boil.
5. Trim, wash, and coarsely grate the zucchini. Stir the zucchini into the soup, and simmer for a further 10 minutes.
6. Taste and adjust the seasoning, if necessary. Pour into individual bowls and serve.
Accompaniment: French bread
Recommended drink: a full-bodied red wine.

CREAM OF BASIL SOUP WITH CHERRY TOMATOES

SERVES 4
Preparation time: 20 minutes
Kcal per serving: 115
P = 4g, F = 8g, C = 8g

1 shallot
1 tbsp butter
2 large, floury potatoes
2 bunches basil
3 cups vegetable broth
3 tbsps Mascarpone
salt
freshly ground white pepper
1 tbsp lemon juice
2 cups cherry tomatoes

1. Peel and finely chop the shallot. Melt the butter in a pan, and gently fry the shallot for 5 minutes until transparent.
2. Peel, wash, and finely dice the potatoes. Add them to the pan, and fry for a further 5 minutes.
3. Wash the basil and shake dry. Set aside a few good leaves for garnishing, and roughly chop the remainder. Add the chopped basil to the pan. Stir in the broth, slowly bring to the boil, and simmer for 15 minutes.
4. Purée the soup in a food processor or with a hand-held mixer, pour through a fine sieve and return to the pan. Stir in the Mascarpone, and season to taste with salt and pepper. Gently heat through, and add the lemon juice.
5. Wash and halve the cherry tomatoes. Pour the soup into deep plates, place the tomatoes in the soup, and garnish with the reserved basil leaves. Chervil makes an excellent alternative to basil.

FISH STEW WITH VEGETABLES AND SAFFRON

SERVES 4
Preparation time: 30 minutes
Kcal per serving: 295
P = 36g, F = 7g, C = 8g

1 onion
2 tbsps butter
4 carrots
2 medium-sized leeks
5 sticks of celery
½ tsp ground saffron
1 cup dry white wine
3 cups fish broth
salt
freshly ground white pepper
juice of ½ lemon
1½ pounds white fish fillets
⅔ cup shrimp

1. Peel and finely chop the onion. Melt the butter in a large skillet, and gently fry the onion for 5 minutes.
2. Peel and thinly slice the carrots. Add to the pan, and gently fry for a further 5 minutes.
3. Trim and wash the leeks. Slice diagonally into pieces ½ inch across.
4. Trim, wash, and thinly slice the celery. Roughly chop the celery leaves. Add the celery and leeks to the pan, and fry for a further 3 minutes.
5. Sprinkle with the saffron, and cook, stirring constantly, for 1 minute. Stir in the white wine and broth, and season to taste with salt and pepper. Stir in 1 tbsp of the lemon juice. Cover and simmer over a medium heat for 15 minutes.

Peel and thinly slice the carrots, using a cucumber slicer, mandolin or sharp knife.

Pour the fish broth over the vegetables, season with salt and pepper, then add lemon juice.

Sprinkle the diced fish with lemon juice, season with salt and pepper and add it to the pan.

6. Wash the fish and pat dry. Cut it into bite-sized pieces. Sprinkle over the remaining lemon juice, and season with salt and pepper. Add the fish and prawns to the pan, and cook over a low heat for 5 minutes. Taste and adjust the seasoning, if necessary, and serve.

> **TIP**
>
> *Vegetable broth may be used instead of fish broth, and the saffron may be replaced by tumeric.*

LEEK STEW WITH SMOKED PORK FILLET

SERVES 4
Preparation time: 30 minutes
Kcal per serving: 400
P = 26g, F = 24g, C = 20g

8 medium potatoes
4 leeks
2 tbsps vegetable oil
1 quart meat broth
14 ounces cooked smoked pork fillet
1 tsp dried marjoram
salt
freshly ground black pepper
1 tbsp red wine vinegar

1. Peel the potatoes and chop into ½-inch cubes.
2. Trim and wash the leeks, and slice into ¼-inch rings.
3. Heat the oil in a pan, and gently fry the potatoes and leeks for 5 minutes. Add the broth and bring to the boil. Cover, lower the heat, and simmer for 10 minutes.

> **TIP**
>
> *Smoked sausage makes an excellent and cheaper alternative to the smoked pork used in this stew.*

4. Meanwhile, cut the pork into ½-inch cubes. Stir the pork into the vegetables.
5. Sprinkle with the marjoram, and season to taste with salt and pepper. Simmer for a further 10 minutes. Stir in the vinegar. Serve hot.

LAMB STEW WITH TOMATOES AND ZUCCHINI

SERVES 4
Preparation time: 30 minutes
Kcal per serving: 435
P = 29g, F = 33g, C = 6g

1½ pounds boned shoulder of lamb
1 large onion, finely chopped
2 tbsps olive oil
salt
freshly ground black pepper
1 tbsp curry powder
1 cup meat broth
2 x 14 ounce-cans peeled tomatoes
8 zucchini
3 garlic cloves
½ tsp ground cumin
1 thyme sprig

1. Wash the meat and pat dry. Cut into ½-inch cubes. Peel and finely chop the onion.
2. Heat the oil in a pan, and fry the meat for 5 minutes over a high heat, stirring frequently. Season to taste with salt, and sprinkle with the curry powder.
3. Stir in the onion, add the broth and add the tomatoes with the can juice. Bring to the boil, and simmer for 25 minutes.
4. Meanwhile, trim, wash, and thinly slice the zucchini.

> **TIP**
>
> *This stew can be made more substantial by the addition of diced potato or rice.*

5. Peel and crush the garlic. Stir it into the stew. Season to taste with salt and pepper, and add the cumin and thyme.
6. Stir in the sliced zucchini 8 minutes before the end of the cooking time. Serve hot.

MIXED MUSHROOM SAUCE

SERVES 4
Preparation time: 30 minutes
Kcal per serving: 85
P = 3g, F = 5g, C = 3g

1 onion
2 tbsps olive oil
2 cups button mushrooms
2 cups oyster mushrooms
3 garlic cloves
1 tsp dried thyme
1 cup tomato juice
salt
freshly ground black pepper
1 tsp sweet paprika
1 tsp balsamic or white wine vinegar
2 tbsps snipped fresh chives

1. Peel and finely chop the onion. Heat the oil in a sauté pan, and gently fry the onion for 5-7 minutes until soft.
2. Meanwhile, wash and thinly slice the button mushrooms. Stir them into the pan.
3. Wash and thinly slice the oyster mushrooms. Add them to the pan, and cook over a medium heat until almost all the liquid has evaporated.
4. Peel and crush the garlic. Sprinkle it over the mushrooms. Sprinkle with the thyme and add the tomato juice. Bring the mixture to the boil.
5. Season to taste with salt, pepper, and stir in the paprika and vinegar.
6. Sprinkle the chives over the mushroom sauce. This sauce goes very well with roast meat or game, pasta and vegetarian dishes, such as vegetable bake.

Stir the sliced button mushrooms into the softened onions.

Thinly slice the oyster mushrooms, and add them to the pan.

Crush the garlic with a garlic press – directly into the pan, if liked.

Sprinkle with the thyme and add the tomato juice.

CHILLED GARLIC AND HERB SAUCE
(photograph page 88/89)

SERVES 4
Preparation time: 15 minutes
Kcal per serving: 220
P = 2g, F = 22g, C = 5g

3 garlic cloves
1 bunch mixed herbs or 5 sprigs each of chives, parsley, dill, and basil
1 bunch chervil
1 bunch sorrel
1 thyme sprig
1 oregano sprig
1 cup thick yogurt
1 egg yolk
3 tbsps olive oil
salt
freshly ground black pepper
freshly grated nutmeg
1 tbsp white wine vinegar
3 tbsps breadcrumbs

1. Peel the garlic cloves. Wash all the herbs and shake dry. Pick the leaves from the stems.
2. Purée the garlic, herbs, yogurt, egg yolk, and olive oil in a food processor.
3. Rub the purée through a sieve, and season to taste with salt, pepper, and nutmeg. Stir in the vinegar.
4. Transfer to a pan, and mix in the breadcrumbs. Simmer for 5 minutes. Stir the mixture thoroughly, taste and adjust the seasoning if necessary. Allow to cool, then place in the refrigerator until ready to serve. This sauce goes well with cooked meat or chicken, boiled eggs, boiled potatoes or simply with a variety of raw vegetables, as a dip.

CHEESE AND NUT SAUCE

SERVES 4
Preparation time: 25 minutes
Kcal per serving: 390
P = 8g, F = 39g, C = 3g

1 cup heavy cream
7 ounces Gorgonzola cheese
4 tbsps ground hazelnuts
salt
freshly ground black pepper
1 garlic clove
1-2 tbsps lemon juice
3 tbsps finely chopped fresh flat-leafed parsley

1. Heat the cream in a pan. Crumble the Gorgonzola. Add it to the pan, and allow to melt over a low heat, stirring occasionally. Simmer the sauce for 3 minutes.
2. As soon as the Gorgonzola has melted completely, stir in the hazelnuts.
3. Season the sauce to taste with salt and pepper. Peel

Add the pieces of Gorgonzola to the warm cream, and melt them over a low heat.

and crush the garlic, and stir it into the sauce. Stir in lemon juice to taste.
4. Sprinkle with the parsley. Serve with pasta or steamed vegetables. A tablespoonful of pickled green peppercorns may be stirred into the sauce in place of the hazelnuts.

GROUND PORK AND SCALLION SAUCE

SERVES 4 ■
Preparation time: 30 minutes
Kcal per serving: 455
P = 20g, F = 38g, C = 7g

1 slice smoked bacon, rind
   removed
1 large onion
1 tbsp olive oil
14 ounces ground pork or
   sausagemeat
salt
freshly ground black pepper
1 tsp dried oregano
1 tsp dried thyme
2 garlic cloves
2 cups canned tomatoes,
   sieved
1 bunch green onions
   (scallions)

1. Finely dice the bacon. Peel and finely chop the onion. Heat the oil in a skillet, and gently fry the bacon for 5-8 minutes until cooked.
2. Add the onion, and fry for a further 5 minutes until transparent.
3. Stir in the pork or sausagemeat, and fry until it becomes crumbly, stirring occasionally and breaking up the meat with a wooden spoon. Season to taste with salt and pepper, and stir in the oregano and thyme. Peel and crush the garlic, and stir it into the pan.
4. Stir in the sieved tomatoes and bring to the boil. Lower the heat and simmer for 10 minutes.
5. Meanwhile, trim, wash and thinly slice the green onions. Taste the sauce and adjust the seasoning, if necessary. Stir in the green onions. This is an excellent accompaniment to pasta, boiled vegetables, potatoes, and bakes.

SWEET-AND-SOUR PLUM SAUCE

SERVES 4 ■
Preparation time: 20 minutes
Kcal per serving: 170
P = 1g, F = 5g, C = 24g

1 onion
2 tbsps sesame oil
⅔ cup dried plums, pitted
1 tsp finely chopped root
   ginger
salt
freshly ground black pepper
1 tsp soy sauce
2 tbsps lemon juice
1 cup dry red wine
1¼ tsps cornstarch

Fresh plums may be used instead of dried ones.

1. Peel and finely chop the onion. Heat the sesame oil, and gently fry the onion for 5-7 minutes.
2. Roughly chop the dried plums. Add the plums and chopped ginger to the pan, and season to taste with salt and pepper.
3. Stir in the soy sauce and lemon juice. Combine the red wine with the cornstarch to make a smooth paste, and stir it into the pan. Slowly bring the mixture to the boil, stirring constantly, and simmer for 3 minutes until the sauce has thickened. Taste and adjust the seasoning, if necessary. Serve as an accompaniment to steak, game, and chicken.

MUSTARD SAUCE

SERVES 4 ■
Preparation time: 25 minutes
Kcal per serving: 270
P = 2g, F = 23g, C = 4g

1 onion
1 tbsp butter
4 tbsps French mustard
½ cup dry white wine
1 cup crème fraîche
salt
freshly ground white pepper
pinch of sugar
dash of lemon juice

1. Peel and finely chop the onion. Melt the butter in a pan, and gently fry the onion for 5-7 minutes.

Lemon juice gives the mustard sauce a pleasantly sharp taste.

2. Stir in the mustard, and add the white wine. Simmer, uncovered, over a medium heat until the liquid has reduced by almost half.
3. Stir in the crème fraîche. Bring to the boil, and season to taste with salt and pepper. Sir in the sugar and lemon juice to taste. Serve with fried or baked fish, steak, or sausages. This sauce also goes well with poached or soft-boiled eggs.

RED WINE SAUCE

SERVES 4 ■
Preparation time: 20 minutes
Kcal per serving: 300
P = 0g, F = 25g, C = 1g

3 shallots
⅔ cup butter
1½ cups dry red wine
salt
freshly ground white pepper
pinch of ground allspice

1. Peel and chop the shallots. Melt 2 tbsps of the butter in a skillet, and gently fry the shallots for 5-7 minutes or until soft. Place the remaining butter in the freezer to chill.

The shallot is a small variety of onion, ideal for delicate sauces.

2. Add the wine to the pan and bring to the boil. Boil, uncovered, over a high heat until the liquid has reduced by at least one-third.
3. Rub the sauce through a fine sieve. Return to the pan and reheat. Season to taste with salt and pepper, and add the allspice.
4. Dice the chilled butter. Beat the butter into the sauce, one piece at a time, with a whisk or a hand mixer. Do not add the next piece until the previous one has been fully incorporated. Do not allow the sauce to boil. This goes very well with steamed fish and with roast or broiled meats.

Microwave Recipes

*T*he recipes in this chapter will satisfy those who not only love soups and stews, but who also have a particular passion for vegetables of all types. A microwave oven enables rapid preparation of the finest vegetable soups and sauces. For the summer, there is Cream of Pea Soup and Fresh Tomato Soup with Basil and Parmesan Cream; while in winter, there is Cream of Celery Soup with Chicken Breast Slices, smooth French Onion Soup, and Curried Cauliflower Soup.
Both sweet and spicy sauces, too, are excellent when prepared in the microwave. All the recipes are extremely easy to follow and make, even for beginners. However, remember to use only containers suitable for the microwave oven. All the standard recipes are for a 600 watt microwave.

Serbian Risotto
(recipe page 110)

CURRIED CAULIFLOWER SOUP

SERVES 4 ■
Standard microwave oven
Preparation time: 35 minutes
Kcal per serving: 130
P = 7g, F = 7g, C = 10g

1 small cauliflower
1 Idaho potato
1 cup milk
2 cups veal broth
salt
freshly ground white pepper
1 tbsp mild curry powder
freshly grated nutmeg
4 tbsps heavy cream
1 egg yolk
2 tbsps chopped parsley

1. Trim and wash the cauliflower, and divide it into small flowerets. Finely chop the stems. Peel and finely dice the potato.
2. Place the cauliflower and potato in a large microwave-safe dish in a layer no more than 1¼ inches deep. Add the milk and broth, and season with salt, pepper, curry powder, and nutmeg. Cover and cook for *16-18 minutes on HIGH*.
3. Remove a few cauliflower flowerets and set them aside. Purée the remaining vegetables with their cooking liquid in a food processor or with a hand-held mixer. Rub the soup through a sieve.
4. Beat together the cream and egg yolk. Beat the egg yolk mixture into the soup, and heat for *2-3 minutes on LOW*, but do not allow it to boil.
5. Pour the soup into individual serving bowls, add the reserved cauliflower flowerets and serve garnished with parsley.

CREAM OF CELERY SOUP WITH CHICKEN BREAST SLICES

SERVES 4 ■■
Standard microwave oven
Preparation time: 45 minutes
Kcal per serving: 190
P = 15g, F = 9g, C = 13g

1 head celery
1 large potato
2 cups chicken broth
1 cup milk
salt
freshly ground white pepper
freshly grated nutmeg
6 ounces skinless chicken
   breast fillet
6 tbsps heavy cream
1 egg yolk
1 tbsp chopped parsley

1. Trim, wash, and dice the celery. Peel and dice the potato. Place the celery, potato, broth and milk in a large microwave-safe dish. Season with salt, pepper and nutmeg. Cover and cook for *25-30 minutes on HIGH*.
2. Wash the chicken breast and pat dry. Season with salt and pepper.
3. Remove the soup from the microwave and place the chicken in the oven. Cook for *2-3 minutes on HIGH*, turning the chicken over halfway through the cooking time.

> ### TIP
>
> *If you wish to omit the chicken, croûtons may be sprinkled over the soup instead.*

4. Purée the celery and potato with the broth in a blender. Rub the mixture through a sieve and return to the microwave-safe dish.
5. Beat together the cream and egg yolk, and stir the mixture into the soup. Place

After about 1 minute of cooking time, turn the chicken over using a pair of tongs, then finish cooking

Stir in the cream and egg yolk mixture, then heat the soup through in the microwave.

in the microwave for *2-3 minutes on LOW*, but do not allow it to boil.
6. Thinly slice the chicken. Serve the soup in deep plates, place the sliced chicken in the middle of each plate, and garnish with the parsley.

FRESH TOMATO SOUP WITH BASIL AND PARMESAN CREAM

SERVES 4 ■
Standard microwave oven
Preparation time: 40 minutes
Kcal per serving: 215
P = 4g, F = 19g, C = 7g

1 onion
2 garlic cloves
4 tbsps olive oil
4 cups ripe tomatoes
salt
freshly ground white pepper
pinch of sugar
1 thyme sprig
1 bayleaf
1½ cups veal broth
10-12 basil leaves
⅓ cup heavy cream
2 tbsps freshly grated
   Parmesan cheese

1. Peel and dice the onion and garlic. Place the onion, garlic, and oil in a microwave-safe dish and cook for *2 minutes on HIGH* until transparent.
2. Meanwhile, wash and chop the tomatoes. Add them to the dish, season to taste with salt and pepper and add the sugar, thyme, and bayleaf. Pour over the stock, cover and cook for *9-12 minutes on HIGH*.
3. Finely chop the basil leaves. Whip the cream until stiff. Stir in the chopped basil and Parmesan cheese.
4. Purée the soup in a blender, rub it through a sieve, and pour it into soup bowls. Place a spoonful of the basil and Parmesan cream in the middle of each bowl.

ENDIVE SOUP WITH SHRIMP

SERVES 4 ■
Standard microwave oven
Preparation time: 30 minutes
Kcal per serving: 210
P = 8g, F = 19g, C = 3g

4 heads endive (Belgiun endive or witloof)
2 shallots
2 tbsps butter or margarine
1½ cups chicken broth
1 cup heavy cream
salt
freshly ground white pepper
pinch of cayenne pepper
1 egg yolk
½ cup shelled, cooked shrimp
2 dill sprigs

1. Trim the endives and cut out the bitter central core. Wash the leaves and cut them into fine strips.
2. Peel and finely dice the shallots. Place the shallots and butter or margarine in a microwave-safe dish and cook for *2-3 minutes on HIGH* until transparent.
3. Add the endive, broth and half the cream, and season with salt, pepper, and cayenne pepper. Cover and cook for *8-10 minutes on HIGH*.
4. Purée half the soup in a food processor or with a hand-held mixer and return it to the dish.
5. Beat together the remaining cream and the egg yolk. Beat the egg yolk mixture into the soup. Stir in the shrimp and return the soup to the microwave, and cook for *2-3 minutes on LOW*.
6. Serve the soup in deep plates, garnished with the dill sprigs.
Diced, cooked ham makes a delicious alternative to the shrimp used in this recipe.

CREAM OF PEA SOUP

SERVES 2-3 ■
Standard microwave oven
Preparation time: 30 minutes
Kcal per serving, serving 2: 330
P = 7g, F = 25g, C = 13g

3 green onions (scallions)
2 tbsps butter or margarine
1 cup shelled young peas
pinch of sugar
salt
freshly ground white pepper
1 cup veal broth
½ cup dry white wine
1 cup heavy cream
8 fresh mint leaves
2 tbsps crème fraîche

1. Trim, wash and thinly slice the green onions. Place the green onions and butter or margarine in a microwave-safe dish and cook for *4 minutes on HIGH* until transparent.
2. Add the peas and sugar, and season to taste with salt and pepper. Pour over the broth, wine, and cream. Cover and cook for *15 minutes on HIGH*.

> ### TIP
> *If you use frozen peas rather than fresh ones, the cooking time must be extended by 3-4 minutes.*

3. Meanwhile, finely chop 4 mint leaves. Stir them into the crème fraîche, and season with salt and pepper.
4. Remove 2 tbsps of the peas from the dish and set aside. Purée the remaining mixture in a food processor or with a hand-held mixer. Rub the soup through a fine sieve, and pour it in soup bowls.

Pour the broth, wine and cream into the peas, seasoned with sugar, salt, and pepper.

Finely chop 4 mint leaves, and stir them into the crème fraîche.

Purée the peas and their cooking liquid thoroughly in a food processor or with a mixer.

5. Place a little of the crème fraîche mixture in the middle of each bowl. Sprinkle over the remaining peas and garnish each bowl with a mint leaf.

FRENCH ONION SOUP

SERVES 2 ■
Standard microwave oven
Preparation time: 20 minutes
Kcal per serving: 370
P = 6g, F = 21g, C = 28g

4 onions
2 tbsps vegetable oil
½ tsp all-purpose flour
salt
freshly ground white pepper
1½ cups strong beef broth
½ cup dry white wine
1 tbsp butter
4 slices French bread
2 tbsps grated Swiss cheese
pinch of sweet paprika

1. Peel and thinly slice the onions and push out into rings. Place the onion rings and oil in a microwave-safe soup tureen and cook for *4-5 minutes on HIGH* until transparent.
2. Sprinkle with the flour, season with salt and pepper, and mix thoroughly. Pour over the broth and the wine, cover and cook for *6-8 minutes on HIGH*.
3. Meanwhile, melt the butter in a non-stick skillet, and fry the French bread slices on both sides until brown and crisp.
4. Place the French bread slices in the soup and sprinkle cheese and paprika on top of the bread. Melt the cheese for *1 minute on HIGH*, or place the soup in the oven or under the broiler until the cheese turns golden-brown. Serve immediately.

SPICY PUSZTA SOUP

SERVES 4 ■
Standard microwave oven
Preparation time: 45 minutes
Kcal per serving: 370
P = 12g, F = 29g, C = 14g

8 ounces bratwurst or
frankfurters
4 onions
2 Idaho potatoes
2 red peppers
3 tbsps vegetable oil
salt
freshly ground black pepper
1 strip of dried chili, crushed
½ tsp ground caraway seeds
½ tsp dried marjoram
1 tbsp sweet paprika
2 tbsps tomato paste
3 cups beef broth
1 tbsp chopped parsley
2 tbsps sour cream

1. Thinly slice the sausages. Peel and dice the onions and potatoes. Halve, seed, wash, and dice the peppers.
2. Place the sausages and onions in a microwave-safe dish, add the oil, and cook for *5-6 minutes on HIGH*.
3. Add the pepper and potatoes, and stir the mixture thoroughly. Season to taste with salt and pepper and add the chili, caraway, marjoram, and paprika. Return the dish to the microwave and cook for *4-5 minutes on HIGH*.
4. Stir in the tomato paste, add the broth, cover and cook for *25-30 minutes on HIGH*.
5. Leave the dish to stand for a short while. Stir in the parsley, and ladle the soup into deep plates. Place a small scoop of sour cream in the middle of each plate before serving.

LENTIL PURÉE SOUP

SERVES 4 ■
Standard microwave oven
Preparation time: 40 minutes
Soaking time: 2-3 hours
Kcal per serving: 425
P = 41g, F = 18g, C = 19g

⅔ cup lentils
1 parsnip
1 carrot
1 onion
1 stick of celery
chicken giblets
1 thyme sprig
1 bayleaf
salt
freshly ground black pepper
pinch of sugar
3 cups water
½ cup dry red wine
2 tbsps red wine vinegar
2 tbsps crème fraîche
½ cup smoked bacon, rind
removed
1 tbsp vegetable oil
1 tbsp chopped parsley

1. Place the lentils in a bowl, cover with cold water, and set aside to soak for 2-3 hours.
2. Peel the parsnip, carrot, and onion. Trim and wash the celery. Wash the chicken giblets. Drain the lentils. Place the lentils, chicken giblets, parsnip, carrot, onion, celery, thyme, and bayleaf in a large microwave-safe dish. Season to taste with salt and pepper, sprinkle with the sugar, and pour over the water. Cover and cook for *10-14 minutes on HIGH*.
3. Remove and discard the chicken giblets. Purée the remaining mixture in a food processor, then rub it through a sieve. Return the mixture to the dish.
4. Stir in the wine, vinegar, and crème fraîche. Cook the soup for *5 minutes on HIGH*.
5. Finely dice the bacon, and place it on a plate with the oil. When the soup is cooked, place the bacon in the microwave oven and

Place the soaked lentils in a microwave-safe dish, together with the chicken and vegetables.

After adding the red wine and red wine vinegar, stir in the crème fraîche.

Chop the bacon very finely, add the oil and cook on HIGH until crisp.

cook for *3-4 minutes on HIGH* and cook until crisp.
6. Ladle the soup into deep plates, and serve garnished with the diced bacon and the parsley.

SWISS CHEESE SOUP WITH WHOLE-WHEAT CROUTONS

SERVES 4 ■ ■
Standard microwave oven
Preparation time: 30 minutes
Kcal per serving: 340
P = 14g, F = 21g, C = 20g

2 shallots
2 tbsps butter or margarine
2 tbsps all-purpose flour
3 cups milk
½ cup white wine
salt
freshly ground white pepper
freshly grated nutmeg
1 large slice of pumpernickel
or rye bread, crusts
removed
⅓ cup Swiss cheese, grated
2 tbsps heavy cream
2 tbsps snipped fresh chives

1. Peel and finely dice the shallots. Place the shallots and butter or margarine in a microwave-safe dish and cook for *2-3 minutes on HIGH* until transparent.
2. Add the flour, stir it in thoroughly, and cook for *1 minute on HIGH*.
3. Stir in the milk and wine, and season with salt, pepper, and nutmeg. Cover and cook for *6-8 minutes on HIGH*.
4. Finely dice the bread and place it on a microwave-safe plate. Remove the soup from the oven, and cook the bread for *2-3 minutes on HIGH*.
5. Stir the cheese into the soup. Lightly whip the cream and set aside. When the bread has turned crisp, remove it from the oven. Return the soup to the oven and cook for *2-3 minutes on LOW* to melt the cheese.
6. Gently stir the cream into the soup. Serve it in bowls and scatter with the rye croûtons and chives.

TRADITIONAL CHICKEN AND EGGPLANT STEW

SERVES 4 ■■

Combination microwave oven
Preparation time: 40 minutes
Standing time: 30 minutes
Kcal per serving: 530
P = 51g, F = 24g, C = 22g

1 large eggplant
salt
freshly ground black pepper
1 frying chicken
4 beefsteak tomatoes
4 Idaho potatoes
1 onion
1 small zucchini
1 red pepper
4 tbsps butter or margarine
1 tbsp sweet paprika
½ cup white wine

1. Trim the eggplant and cut it into ¼-inch thick slices. Place in a colander and sprinkle generously with salt. Set aside for about 30 minutes to degorge.
2. Soak an unpluged earthenware pot (a chicken brick) in water.
3. Wash and dry the chicken, and divide it into 8 portions. Season with salt and pepper.
4. Rinse the tomatoes with water, then place them in a microwave-safe container while still wet. Cover and heat in the microwave for 3-4 minutes on HIGH. Rinse with cold water, skin, seed, and chop the flesh.
5. Peel and thinly slice the potatoes and onion. Trim, wash and thinly slice the zucchini.
6. Halve, seed, and wash the pepper, and cut into matchstick strips.
7. Melt half the butter and brushit over the earthenware dish. Rinse the eggplant, pat dry, and press flat. Mix together the tomatoes, potatoes, onion, zucchini, pepper and eggplant, and place them in the prepared

Soak the earthenware dish in water, then brush it thoroughly with melted butter.

Arrange the chicken pieces on the pre-cooked eggplant and other vegetables.

dish. Season to taste with salt and pepper, and sprinkle with half the paprika. Cover and cook in the microwave for *15 minutes on HIGH,* stirring occasionally.
8. Remove the dish and heat the oven to a conventional setting of 500°F.
9. Uncover the dish, add the wine and arrange the chicken on top. Dot with the remaining butter, and sprinkle over the remaining paprika. Cook uncovered for *18-22 minutes on HIGH and 500°F (450°F for fan-assisted ovens).* Leave to stand briefly, then serve in the earthenware pot.

Recommended wine: dry white wine.

SERBIAN RISOTTO
(photograph page 102/103)

SERVES 2 ■

Standard microwave oven
Preparation time: 30 minutes
Kcal per serving: 470
P = 34g, F = 15g, C = 50g

1 onion
1 garlic clove
1 yellow pepper
1 red pepper
1 green pepper
2 tomatoes
8 ounces boneless leg of pork
salt
freshly ground black pepper
2 tbsps olive oil
½ cup long-grain rice
1 strip of dried chili, crushed
1 tsp sweet paprika
1 tsp tomato paste
1 cup beef sbroth
1 tbsp chopped fresh parsley

1. Peel and finely dice the onion and garlic. Halve, seed, and wash the peppers and finely dice.
2. Rinse the tomatoes with water, then place in a microwave-safe container while still wet. Cover and heat in the microwave for *2-3 minutes on HIGH.* Rinse with cold water, skin, seed and chop the flesh.
3. Wash the meat and pat dry. Cut into ½-inch cubes, and season with salt and pepper.
4. Place the onion, garlic, and oil in a microwave-safe dish and cook for *3-4 minutes on HIGH* until transparent.
5. Add the peppers, meat, tomatoes, rice, and chili, and season with salt, pepper. and paprika. Stir in the tomato paste and add the broth. Cover and cook for *10 minutes on HIGH and a further 15 minutes on DEFROST.*
6. Leave to stand for a short while, then stir the risotto thoroughly, and serve garnished with parsley.

Peppers are rich in vitamins and also add color to any dish.

Using a sharp meat knife, cut the meat into ½-inch cubes.

Season the meat and vegetable mixture, add the tomato paste and add the broth.

Recommended drink: a fruity rosé wine or lager.

BÉCHAMEL SAUCE

SERVES 4
Standard microwave oven
Preparation time: 10 minutes
Kcal per serving: 160
P = 5g, F = 11g, C = 11g

2 tbsps butter or margarine
2 tbsps all-purpose flour
2 cups milk
salt
freshly ground white pepper
freshly grated nutmeg
dash of lemon juice

Stir the flour into the melted butter or margarine with a whisk.

Stir the milk into the heated flour and butter or margarine mixture.

1. Place the butter or margarine in a microwave-safe dish and melt for *1 minute on HIGH.*
2. Stir in the flour, and cook for a further *1 minute on HIGH.*
3. Stir in the milk, and cook, uncovered, for *4-5 minutes on HIGH,* stirring thoroughly two or three times. Season with salt and pepper, and stir in nutmeg and lemon juice to taste. Use as an accompaniment to vegetables.

SWEET-AND-SOUR MANGO SAUCE

SERVES 2
Standard microwave oven
Preparation time: 15 minutes
Kcal per serving: 185
P = 1g, F = 10g, C = 22g

1 small ripe mango
2 shallots
2 tbsps oil
½ tsp freshly grated root
    ginger
pinch of ground coriander
    (cilanto)
1 tsp mild curry powder
1 strip of dried chili, crushed
1 tsp clear honey
2 tbsps soy sauce
2 tbsps medium sherry
juice of ½ orange
salt
freshly ground black pepper

1. Peel the mango, slice the flesh away from the stone and chop finely. Peel and finely dice the shallots.
2. Place the mango, shallots, oil, ginger, coriander, curry powder, chili, honey, soy sauce, sherry, and orange juice in a microwave-safe dish, and season to taste with salt and pepper. Cover and cook for *8-10 minutes on HIGH,* stirring once during cooking. Serve as an accompaniment to rice or broiled meats or fish.

> **TIP**
>
> *You can serve the sauce as it is with the chopped fruit, or purée it in a food processor.*

CRANBERRY AND ORANGE SAUCE

SERVES 4
Standard microwave oven
Preparation time: 20 minutes
Kcal per serving: 140
P = 0g, F = 0g, C = 29g

1 cup fresh cranberries
⅓ cup dry red wine
½ cup sugar
grated rind and juice of
    1 orange
2 cloves
1 stick of cinnamon

1. Pick over and wash the cranberries. Drain.
2. Place the cranberries, wine, sugar, orange rind, orange juice, cloves, and cinnamon in a microwave-safe dish. Cover and cook for *8 minutes on HIGH* and a further *4-5 minutes on LOW,* stirring occasionally.
3. Remove and discard the cloves and the cinnamon

Interrupt the cooking process briefly to stir the cranberry and orange sauce.

stick. Purée the sauce in a food processor. Serve as an accompaniment to vanilla ice cream, pancakes, or with baked desserts. This sauce is also delicious cold with roast beef or game.

BOLOGNESE SAUCE

SERVES 4
Standard microwave oven
Preparation time: 40 minutes
Kcal per serving: 220
P = 13g, F = 13g, C = 5g

1 onion
1-2 garlic cloves
1 large carrot
2 sticks of celery
3 tbsps olive oil
7 ounces mixed ground
    meats
1¾ cups canned chopped
    tomatoes
½ cup dry red wine
1 cup beef broth
salt
freshly ground black pepper
2 thyme sprigs
1 rosemary sprig
4 tbsps heavy cream
1 tbsp chopped fresh parsley

1. Peel and finely chop the onion and garlic. Peel and finely dice the carrot. Trim, wash, and finely dice the celery.
2. Place the onion, garlic, carrot, celery, and oil in a large microwave-safe dish. Cook for *4-5 minutes on HIGH.*
3. Add the ground meat and the tomatoes. Add the wine and broth, season to taste with salt and pepper, and add the thyme and rosemary. Cover and cook for *15-18 minutes on HIGH.*
4. Stir in the cream. Cook, uncovered, for a further *5 minutes on HIGH.*
5. Remove and discard the thyme and rosemary. Stir in the chopped parsley and serve hot as an accompaniment to spaghetti or gnocchi.

Lean Cuisine

The days are long since over when anyone trying to lose weight or even merely aiming to keep their weight stable had to steer clear of nourishing soups and spicy stews. Labeling such dishes as "fattening" was quite unjustified, as they can also be made light and low in calories. Anyone sampling *Cream of Zucchini Soup with Pumpkin Seeds* would certainly not feel as if he or she were on a diet – even with only 80 calories per serving. Being slim need not mean economizing on taste and quality, and this is demonstrated time and again by the numerous chilled soups made with all types of fruits, and the light sauces described in this section.

Chinese Vegetable Soup with
Chicken
(recipe page 118)

115

POTATO SOUP WITH WATERCRESS

SERVES 2 ■

Preparation time: 30 minutes
Kcal per serving: 155
P = 3g, F = 9g, C = 15g

2 Idaho potatoes
1 bunch watercress
1 shallot
1 tbsp butter
freshly ground white pepper
1⅔ cup chicken broth

1. Peel and dice the potatoes.
2. Trim and wash the watercress. Set aside the tender top leaves for the garnish and chop the remainder.
3. Peel and dice the shallot.
4. Melt the butter in a skillet, and gently fry the shallot for 5 minutes. Add the potatoes and half the chopped watercress, and fry for a further 5

Trim and wash the watercress and finely chop the leaves.

minutes. Season to taste with salt and pepper.
5. Add the broth, bring to the boil and cook for about 15 minutes. Add the remaining chopped watercress, and cook for a further 5 minutes.
6. Purée the soup with a hand-held mixer or in a food processor. Pour into individual soup bowls and garnish with the reserved watercress.

KOHLRABI SOUP WITH GROUND VEAL SPAETZLE

SERVES 4 ■ ■

Preparation time: 45 minutes
Kcal per serving: 245
P = 8g, F = 16g, C = 7g

2 kohlrabi
1 onion
1 tbsp butter
salt
freshly ground white pepper
freshly grated nutmeg
3 cups veal broth
1 cup wine

FOR THE GROUND VEAL SPAETZLE:
6 ounces ground veal
1 small egg
1 tsp breadcrumbs
salt
freshly ground white pepper
1 tsp chopped fresh parsley
grated rind of ½ lemon

1. Peel the kohlrabi, setting aside the tender inner leaves. Slice the root and cut into matchstick strips.
2. Peel and finely chop the onion. Melt the butter in a skillet, and gently fry the onion for 5 minutes until it is transparent.
3. Add the kohlrabi, and fry for a further 5 minutes. Season with salt, pepper, and nutmeg, and add the broth and wine. Cover and cook for about 15 minutes.
4. To make the spaetzle, mix together the ground veal and egg. Add the breadcrumbs, and stir thoroughly until the mixture is smooth. Season to taste with salt and pepper. Stir in the parsley and lemon rind.
5. Purée half the kohlrabi soup with a hand-held mixer or in a food processor. Return the purée to the pan and heat the soup through.
6. Press the ground veal mixture through a sieve, or scrape small pieces of the mixture from a wooden board straight into the soup.

Kohlrabi is a member of the cabbage family; the root, rather than the leaves, is used in cooking

Peel the kohlrabi, slice and then cut into matchstick strips.

Purée half the kohlrabi soup with a hand-held mixer or in a food processor.

Boil for a few minutes. Finely chop the reserved kohlrabi leaves. Ladle the soup into 4 individual soup bowls and garnish with the kohlrabi leaves. To make this soup spicier and more filling, use spicy sausagemeat for the spaetzle.

SPINACH SOUP WITH CHEESE CROÛTONS

SERVES 4 ■ ■

Preparation time: 35 minutes
Kcal per serving: 180
P = 8g, F = 12g, C = 10g

6 cups young spinach
1 small onion
1 garlic clove
3 tbsps butter or margarine
salt
freshly ground white pepper
freshly grated nutmeg
2 cups veal broth
1 cup skimmed milk
2 slices white bread, crusts removed
2 tbsps grated Parmesan cheese

1. Trim, wash, and drain the spinach leaves. Peel and mince the onion and garlic.
2. Melt half the butter in a large skillet, and gently fry the onion and garlic until transparent. Add the spinach and cook for 3-4 minutes.
3. Season with salt, pepper, and nutmeg, and add the broth and milk. Cover and simmer for about 15-20 minutes.
4. Purée the soup with a hand-held mixer or in a food processor, rub it through a sieve and return to the pan. Bring back to the boil.
5. Meanwhile, dice the bread. Melt the remaining butter in a non stick skillet, and fry the bread cubes on all sides over a medium heat until golden-brown. Sprinkle with the cheese and fry until the bread is coated with melted cheese, stirring constantly with a wooden spoon.
6. Ladle the soup into heated soup bowls or plates and garnish with the cheese croûtons.

CHINESE VEGETABLE SOUP WITH CHICKEN

(photograph page 114/115)

SERVES 4 ■■
Preparation time: 45 minutes
Soaking time: 3-4 hours
Kcal per serving: 150
P = 11g, F = 7g, C = 7g

1 tbsp dried Chinese
    mushrooms
1 small leek
1 large carrot
1-2 garlic cloves
2 tbsps peanut oil
6 ounces skinless chicken
    breast fillet
salt
freshly ground white pepper
1 tsp grated root ginger
pinch of cayenne pepper
1 quart chicken broth
2 tbsps soy sauce
3 tbsps rice wine or dry
    sherry
1 ounce transparent noodles
1 tbsp chopped parsley

1. Place the mushrooms in a small bowl, cover with luke-warm water, and set aside for 3-4 hours to soak.
2. Trim, wash, and thinly slice the leek. Peel and thinly slice the carrot. Peel and finely chop the garlic.
3. Heat the oil in a skillet, and fry the chicken for 3-4 minutes on each side. Remove from the pan, cover, and set aside.
4. Squeeze out the mushrooms and chop them finely. Gently fry the leek, carrot, garlic, and mushrooms in the hot oil for 5 minutes. Season to taste with salt and pepper, add the ginger and cayenne pepper, and add the broth, soy sauce and rice wine or sherry. Bring soup to the boil, and simmer for about 10 minutes over a medium heat.
5. Snip the transparent noodles. Dice the chicken. Stir the noodles and chicken into the soup and simmer gently for a further 4-5 minutes.

Chicken broth can be made by boiling chicken trimmings and soup vegetables in lightly salted water.

Gently fry the chicken breast in the oil, on both sides, then fry the vegetables and mushrooms.

Snip the raw transparent noodles with a pair of kitchen scissors, and cut the cooked chicken into bite-sized pieces.

6. Taste and adjust the seasoning, if necessary. Pour the soup into bowls and garnish with chopped parsley. Small meat dumplings may be added to the soup as an alternative to chicken.

TOMATO SOUP WITH FRIED TOFU

SERVES 4 ■■
Preparation time: 45 minutes
Kcal per serving: 115
P = 6g, F = 8g, C = 7g

4 cups tomatoes
1 onion
1 garlic clove
1 thyme sprig
1 oregano sprig
salt
freshly ground black pepper
2 cups water
1 cup tofu
2 tbsps olive oil
6-8 basil leaves

1. Wash and dice the tomatoes. Peel and dice the onion and garlic. Place the tomatoes, onion, garlic, thyme, and oregano in a pan, season to taste with salt and pepper and add the water. Cover and simmer over a medium heat for about 20 minutes.
2. Rub the mixture through a sieve and adjust the seasoning, if necessary. Return to the pan.
3. Cut the tofu into ¾-inch cubes. Heat the oil in a nonstick skillet, and fry the tofu all over, stirring frequently, until golden-brown.
4. Tear the basil leaves into strips. Add the basil and tofu to the tomato soup, heat through and serve.

CREAM OF ZUCCHINI SOUP WITH PUMPKIN SEEDS

SERVES 2 ■
Preparation time: 35 minutes
Kcal per serving: 235
P = 3g, F = 12g, C = 8g

2 small zucchini
1 shallot
1 garlic clove
1 tbsp oil
salt
freshly ground white pepper
1 cup dry white wine
1 cup chicken broth
2 tbsps pumpkin seeds
2 tbsps heavy cream

1. Trim, wash, and slice the zucchini. Peel and finely chop the shallot and garlic.
2. Heat the oil in a skillet, and gently fry the shallot and garlic for 5 minutes. Add the zucchini, and fry for a further 5 minutes. Season to taste with salt and pepper.

> **TIP**
>
> *The pumpkin seeds may be replaced by croûtons or sunflower seeds.*

3. Add the wine and stock, cover and simmer for about 15 minutes over a medium heat.
4. Dry-fry the pumpkin seeds in a nonstick skillet.
5. Purée the zucchini soup finely with a hand-held mixer or in a food processor, then rub it through a sieve. Adjust the seasoning, if necessary. Whip the cream, and gently fold into the soup.
6. Serve the soup in deep plates and sprinkle with the pumpkin seeds.

CHILLED CUCUMBER SOUP WITH BAY SHRIMP

SERVES 4
Preparation time: 20 minutes
Kcal per serving: 90
P = 8g, F = 3g, C = 8g

1 cucumber
2 garlic cloves
1 cup yogurt
salt
freshly ground white pepper
pinch of cayenne pepper
½ yellow pepper
½ red pepper
½ green pepper
1 shallot
½ cup peeled, cooked bay shrimp
1 tbsp finely chopped dill

1. Peel the cucumber, cut it in half, and scoop out the seeds with a spoon. Chop the flesh.
2. Peel the garlic. Place the garlic, cucumber, and yogurt in a food processor and purée. Alternatively, purée with a hand-held mixer. Season to taste with salt, pepper, and cayenne pepper. Chill in the refrigerator.

> **TIP**
>
> *Diced tomato or finely chopped celery also taste superb in this cold cucumber soup.*

3. Seed, wash, and finely dice the peppers. Peel and finely dice the shallot. Mix the peppers and shallot together.
4. Serve the chilled cucumber soup in deep plates or bowls, place the diced vegetables in the middle of each and garnish with the shrimp and dill.

EXOTIC CHILLED FRUIT SOUP

SERVES 4
Preparation time: 25 minutes
Kcal per serving: 110
P = 2g, F = 1g, C = 22g

1 large, ripe mango
1 ripe papaya
1 cup freshly squeezed orange juice
½ cup freshly squeezed grapefruit juice
1 tbsp orange liqueur
sweetener to taste
½ starfruit (carambola)
1 tbsp chopped pistachio nuts

1. Peel the mango and papaya. Cut the mango flesh

Peel the mango and papaya, cut the mango flesh from the stone, and scoop the seeds from the papaya, then purée the flesh.

away from the stone by slicing thinly towards the center. Halve the papaya and scoop out the black seeds with a spoon.
2. Purée the mango and papaya flesh in a food processor. Stir in the orange and grapefruit juice. Add the orange liqueur and sweetener to taste.
3. Wash and thinly slice the star fruit (carambola).
4. Ladle the fruit soup into deep plates, decorate with the starfruit slices, and sprinkle with the nuts. Serve ice-cold.

CHILLED GOOSEBERRY SOUP WITH KIWI FRUITS

(photograph page 23)

SERVES 4
Preparation time: 20 minutes
Kcal per serving: 70
P = 1g, F = 0g, C = 15g

3 cups canned gooseberries
½ vanilla pod
1 strip of lemon rind
3 cups water
2 kiwi fruits
sweetener to taste

1. Split the vanilla pod lengthwise. Place the goose-

Peel and slice the kiwi fruits.

berries, vanilla pod, lemon rind and water in a pan. Bring to the boil, and cook until the gooseberries are soft and have split open.
2. Peel the kiwi fruits. Slice 1 kiwi fruit crosswise, and set it aside. Cut the other kiwi fruits in half.
3. Purée the gooseberries with their cooking liquid and the halved kiwi fruits in a food processor, then rub the mixture through a sieve. Add sweetener to taste, place the soup in the refrigerator.
4. Ladle the soup into deep plates, arrange the kiwi fruit slices on top and serve well chilled.

ICED MELON SOUP WITH RASPBERRIES

SERVES 4
Preparation time: 15 minutes
Kcal per serving: 130
P = 2g, F = 1g, C = 9g

1 small Persian melon
1 cup fruity white wine
juice and rind of 1 lime
sweetener to taste
1 cup raspberries
a few ice cubes
4 mint sprigs

1. Halve the melon and scoop out the seeds with a spoon.
2. Using a melon baller, scoop out 12 small balls of flesh and place them in the refrigerator. Peel the melon halves and purée the remaining flesh with the wine in a food processor. Stir in the lime juice, lime rind, and sweetener to taste.
3. Wash and hull the raspberries.

> **TIP**
>
> *Very ripe loganberries make a delicious alternative to the raspberries. Persian melons are particularly juicy, sweet, and aromatic. They are, therefore, especially suitable for this recipe.*

4. Place the ice cubes in a plastic bag and crush them with a steak hammer or rolling pin. Arrange the crushed ice in a bowl.
5. Stir the melon balls and raspberries into the melon purée, and transfer the mixture to the bowl of crushed ice. Garnish with the mint leaves.

INDIAN-STYLE ONION SAUCE

SERVES 4 ■

Preparation time: 20 minutes
Kcal per serving: 90
P = 1g, F = 6g, C = 8g

1 large onion
1 garlic clove
2 tbsps sesame oil
1 banana
1 tsp mild curry powder
1 tsp freshly grated root
  ginger
pinch of cayenne pepper
pinch of ground cinnamon
salt
freshly ground white pepper
1 cup chicken broth
2 tbsps low-fat yogurt

1. Peel and finely dice the onion and garlic.
2. Heat the oil in a nonstick skillet, and gently fry the onion and garlic until transparent.
3. Peel and dice the banana. Add the banana, curry powder, ginger, cayenne pepper, and cinnamon to the pan. Season to taste with salt and pepper, and add the broth.

Gently fry the finely chopped onion and garlic in the sesame oil until transparent.

4. Bring the mixture to the boil, and cook over a medium heat for about 5 minutes until the sauce is creamy. If liked, it may be puréed in a food processor.
5. Stir in the yogurt. Serve as an accompaniment to rice and roast meats or fish.

MEAT SAUCE WITH GREEN PEPPERCORNS

SERVES 4 ■

Preparation time: 25 minutes
Kcal per serving: 235
P = 23g, F = 12g, C = 3g

1 onion
1 garlic clove
1 slice smoked bacon, rind
  removed
1 tbsp vegetable oil
1¾ cups finely ground lean
  beef
salt
1 tbsp Dijon mustard
2 tbsps pickled green
  peppercorns
½ cup dry white wine
1 cup beef broth
2 tbsps heavy cream
1 beefsteak tomato
2 tbsps finely chopped fresh
  parsley (optional)

1. Peel and finely chop the onion and garlic. Finely dice the bacon.
2. Heat the oil in a nonstick skillet, and gently fry the onion, garlic, and bacon for 5 minutes.
3. Add the ground beef, and fry for 6-7 minutes, stirring occasionally. Season to taste with salt, and stir in the mustard and peppercorns. Add the wine and broth, and boil over a high heat to reduce the liquid.
4. Add the cream, and boil for a further 2-3 minutes.
5. Blanch, skin, and seed the tomato, and finely dice the flesh. Stir the tomato into the sauce, and bring back to the boil. If liked, sprinkle over the chopped parsley. The sauce may be varied by using capers instead of green peppercorns. Serve as an accompaniment to pasta or boiled potatoes.

SLIMMING GREEN SAUCE

SERVES 4 ■

Preparation time: 15 minutes
Kcal per serving: 70
P = 4g, F = 4g, C = 3g

2 shallots
1-2 garlic cloves
1 hard-boiled egg
1 large picked gherkin
3 tbsps chopped mixed fresh
  herbs (e.g. parsley, chives,
  chervil, basil, tarragon,
  sorrel)
1 tsp Dijon mustard
1 tbsp tarragon vinegar
1 cup yogurt
2 tbsps crème fraîche
salt
freshly ground white pepper

1. Peel and finely chop the shallots and garlic. Shell and finely chop the egg. Dice the gherkin. Thoroughly mix together the shallots, garlic, egg, and gherkin.
2. Stir in the herbs, mustard, vinegar, yogurt, and crème fraîche, and season to taste with salt and pepper. Finely chopped pickled red pepper or finely chopped mixed pickles may also be added. Serve as an accompaniment to boiled or roast beef.

> **TIP**
>
> *It is essential to use fresh herbs for the sauce.*

SHIITAKE MUSHROOM SAUCE

SERVES 2 ■ ■

Preparation time: 30 minutes
Kcal per serving: 260
P = 5g, F = 25g, C = 5g

1 onion
1 carrot
1 slice smoked bacon, rind
  removed
1 cup shiitake mushrooms
1 tbsp butter
salt
freshly ground black pepper
⅓ cup beef broth
⅓ cup dry white wine
1 tbsp crème fraîche
1 tbsp chopped fresh parsley

1. Peel and chop the onion. Peel and finely dice the carrot. Finely dice the bacon. Wash and finely chop the mushrooms.
2. Melt the butter in a nonstick skillet, and gently fry the onion, carrot, and bacon for about 5 minutes over a medium heat until the onion is soft.

Wash and finely chop the shiitake mushrooms.

3. Add the mushrooms and gently fry for a further 3-4 minutes. Season to taste with salt and pepper. Add the broth and wine, and bring to the boil over a high heat to reduce some of the liquid.
4. Stir in the crème fraîche, and boil the sauce until it turns creamy. Serve garnished with parsley.

Index